PLURAL SOCIETIES
AND NEW STATES

Plural Societies and New States

A CONCEPTUAL ANALYSIS

ROBERT JACKSON

Institute of International Studies
University of California, Berkeley

International Standard Book Number 0-87725-130-4
Library of Congress Card Number 77-620004

Plural Societies and New States

A CONCEPTUAL ANALYSIS

ROBERT JACKSON

Institute of International Studies
University of California, Berkeley

International Standard Book Number 0-87725-130-4
Library of Congress Card Number 77-620004
© 1977 by the Regents of the University of California

ACKNOWLEDGMENTS

This study attempts to apply the conceptual and linguistic methods of contemporary political theory to the analysis of
government in underdeveloped countries. I am grateful to
Reinhard Bendix, Robert Biller, and R.S. Milne, as well as the
anonymous readers of the Institute of International Studies,
for helpful comments on an earlier version. I would also
like to thank Carl G. Rosberg, Director of the Institute, for
his advice and encouragement, and the staff of the Institute
for their assistance. Paul Gilchrist, Editor of the Institute,
deserves special thanks for the efforts he has made to improve
the quality of the text. Finally, I want to thank the Canada
Council for a Leave Fellowship in support of this study.

R.J.

November 1976
Vancouver, Canada

CONTENTS

Chapter I

INTRODUCTION

In the past quarter century there has been an extraor-
dinary growth of academic interest in the new states. The
anti-colonial revolution that has created so many new Asian and
African countries has set off an "academic revolution" of sorts
that has altered markedly the shape and content of several
social science disciplines. The effects of this academic change
have been particularly noticeable in political science, and most
particularly in the subfield of "comparative politics."

When the movement for national independence from Western
colonialism began to meet with widespread success in the 1950's,
political science responded by turning its attention to the
enlarging universe of political life. Not entirely coincidental-
ly, at about this time a growing confidence in the empirical and
scientific credentials of political science was being registered.
In comparative politics these changes were reflected in the ap-
pearance of Gabriel Almond and James Coleman's The Politics of
the Developing Areas in 1960--the year which also marked the
watershed of independence in tropical Africa. This book, perhaps
more than any other single publication, signified the emergence
of comparative politics as a global field of study with corres-
ponding methods and approach. It was an approach, as Reinhard
Bendix observed at the time, which considered politics to be a
"universal phenomenon," and which deduced from this the need to
find universal categories and concepts of analysis "to comprise
in one conceptual scheme all political phenomena, Western and
non-Western."[1] Bendix called attention to some remarks by Almond
which conveyed something of the reforming spirit of the new
comparative politics movement:

> We are not setting aside public law and philosophy as
> disciplines, but simply telling them to move over to make
> room for a growth in political theory that has been long
> overdue.[2]

---

[1]Reinhard Bendix, "Social Stratification and the Political
Community" in Peter Laslett and W.G. Runciman, eds., Philosophy,
Politics and Society (2nd ser.; Oxford: Basil Blackwell, 1962),
p. 228.

[2]Gabriel Almond and James S. Coleman, eds., The Politics of

However, I believe that it is more accurate to say that public law and philosophy were being fairly well set aside by comparative political studies. The disenchantment with institutional and philosophical studies occurred, somewhat ironically, at a time when a new turn was being taken by contemporary legal and political theory, and when a rediscovery of a more institutional and historical sociology was being made. On the one hand, a precise and discriminating kind of "analytic" political theory was being developed partly under the influence of new methods of linguistic analysis that were being fashioned by British and American philosophers,[3] and partly in reaction to pronouncements by positivists--most notably by T.D. Weldon--that normative political theory was for all intents and purposes quite "dead." On the other hand, Max Weber was being reinterpreted and extensively translated into English, and a renewed interest in the institutional and philosophical approaches of other nineteenth- and early twentieth-century sociologists and social theorists was underway.[4] In their separate ways, both of these intellectual developments rekindled interest in refining and using the inherited stock of established legal, political, and social concepts rather than inventing new ones.

In recent years, however, there has been considerable evidence of a revival of interest in historical sociology among comparativists--particularly in Weber's writings dealing with "patrimonialism" and related concepts and in the general sociology of patron-client relationships. The utility of these and related

---

the Developing Areas (Princeton: Princeton University Press, 1960), p. 4.

[3]This linguistic turn in modern philosophy is recorded particularly well in Richard Rorty, ed., The Linguistic Turn: Recent Essays in Philosophical Method (Chicago: University of Chicago Press, 1967), and in political theory in the series Philosophy, Politics and Society, edited by P. Laslett and W.G. Runciman.

[4]The reinterpretation of Max Weber is probably best represented by Reinhard Bendix, Max Weber: An Intellectual Portrait (New York: Anchor Books, 1962); Max Weber, Economy and Society: An Outline of Interpretive Sociology, ed. Guenther Roth and Claus Wittich (3 vols.; New York: Bedminster Press, 1968); and Reinhard Bendix and Guenther Roth, Scholarship and Partisanship: Essays on Max Weber (Berkeley: University of California Press, 1971). The reevaluation of nineteenth- and early twentieth-century social theory is well represented by Raymond Aron, Main Currents in Sociological Thought (2 vols.; New York: Basic Books, 1965), and Robert Nisbet, The Sociological Tradition (London: Heinemann, 1966).

concepts in the political analysis of underdeveloped countries has been widely remarked upon. Regrettably, there has been little evidence as yet of any serious interest by comparativists in the recent analytical discoveries made by philosophers and political theorists. I say "regrettably" because I believe that the concepts and analytical tools the philosophers and political theorists have been working with can be used to sharpen our understanding of the many, often subtle, normative distinctions and conflicts between the "developed" and the "underdeveloped" political conditions. By borrowing their tools and concepts I believe that we can begin the neglected enterprise of accurately mapping the meandering boundary that separates the new states from the old societies upon which they have been imposed. This boundary can be defined--provisionally--as the points of tension and conflict between the institutional rules and standards of the new state and those of the old society. In the analysis of such normative tensions and conflicts, institutional and philosophical approaches have always seemed the most appropriate.

An institutional and normative analysis--"normative" in the sense of being interested in norms but most certainly not in prescribing them--will reveal many examples of such conflicts in contemporary underdeveloped countries, including conflicts between national citizenship and communal membership, between the general public interest and the communal interest, between official duty and social obligation, between national identity and parochial or local sentiment. These points of tension and conflict have been explored from the sociological perspective in an admirable study edited by Clifford Geertz and published under the title Old Societies and New States.[5] There have been numerous other (though I believe less valuable) sociological studies of the boundary since the Geertz work appeared, but the boundary has not been explored, so far as I am aware, from the perspective of modern analytic political theory.[6] My primary aim is to initiate such an inquiry.

That such tensions and conflicts are essentially conflicts of competing conceptions of right and proper conduct--of competing norms--is revealed perhaps most clearly in the analysis of patronage and corruption in government in underdeveloped countries. Indeed, this study originated in my dissatisfaction with those (often functional) studies that suggest that corruption, for instance, always must be viewed unambiguously as deviant behavior.

---

[5]New York: The Free Press, 1963.

[6]One very valuable study that inclines in this direction is Carl Landé, Leaders, Factions and Parties (Monograph Series, No. 6, Southeast Asia Studies, Yale University, 1966).

Of course, conceptually it is deviant behavior, but this does not answer the comparative analytical question, which is: "From what social norm or standard is it deviant?" The unsatisfactory answer almost invariably provided by such studies is that the behavior is deviant from the "modern" standards of the new state. In this study, I suggest (among other things) that deviance from such norms may be conformance with others--that what from the modern viewpoint of public government must necessarily be considered "corrupt" conduct may from another viewpoint (say that of a communal group in the old society) be considered normal and acceptable.

To analyze and evaluate political conduct in contemporary underdeveloped countries from the perspective of the new state only is to invite the serious possibility of misconception and, hence, misunderstanding. I would suggest that if a normative word like "corruption" is liable to be mishandled in comparative analysis, so also are other normative words such as "law," "policy," "regulation," "duty," "responsibility," and so on. Since a word like "corruption" (wrong conduct) is logically connected, sometimes directly and sometimes indirectly, with words like "rule" or "regulation" (standard of conduct), then if circumspection and caution are required in the use of the former, they will also be required in the uses of the latter. The point of such care when employing the vocabulary of politics and government in comparative analysis is not to engage in nit-picking or hair-splitting: it is rather to increase the power and perception of our analysis--to provide, in the words of Raymond Williams, "that extra edge of consciousness."[7] The secondary aim is to show what we might stand to gain from such a method of analysis.

By subjecting some of the oft-noted characteristics and practices of government in underdeveloped countries to a careful conceptual analysis, I shall attempt to show why the condition of political "underdevelopment" should be conceived as a dis-tinctive kind of polity in its own right: one that not only deviates from the norms and standards of the new state but also conforms with an alternative set of norms and standards that are rarely conceived of as such by comparative political scien-tists. I shall argue that such a polity is a distinctive institutional order with its own normative theory. My task is to define some elements of this theory and to sketch (regrettably all too vaguely) an outline of them. This then is a conceptual rather than an empirical study. It is concerned with ways of

---

[7]Keywords: A Vocabulary of Culture and Society (New York: Oxford University Press, 1976), p. 21.

4

conceiving a type of polity that we would ordinarily describe as a pluralistic society with a highly personal and apparently corrupt form of government. The evidence is overwhelming that there are many such polities in what has come to be known as the Third World.

Chapter II

PLURALISM

Two Theories of Pluralism

The modern literature of political science and sociology includes two main theories of pluralism: a _political_ theory of the Western "plural polity" and a _sociological_ theory of the non-Western "plural society." The first theory was developed in the analysis of the Western constitutional state--particularly the Anglo-American democracies and, most specifically, the American polity.[8] The second was developed in the analysis of colonial societies.[9] Since many newly independent states are often described as "pluralist," it is essential to examine these two theories of pluralism to see how they can aid (or hinder) a normative analysis of government in such countries.

The political theory of Western pluralism is first of all a revisionist theory of the state that takes issue with the idea of sovereignty advanced by Hobbes and Austin. It is critical of a concept of the state as a "determinate person or body of persons" capable of securing habitual obedience from its non-sovereign members. For Austin the doctrine of sovereignty suggests a concept of law as "general orders" or "commands" backed by sanctions issued by an agent or agency "habitually" obeyed. The pluralist criticism is to observe, with H.L.A. Hart, that many laws are not coercive orders or commands.[10] Laws, as well

---

[8] The political theory combines a "normative" approach associated with the English pluralists (Figgis, Cole, Laski, and Barker, to mention the leading figures) and an analytical approach that has come to be identified with the American political science "establishment." For a helpful review, see J. Roland Pennock and John Chapman, eds., _Nomos XI: Voluntary Association_ (New York: Atherton Press, 1969).

[9] The sociological theory was originated by J.S. Furnivall (_Netherlands India_ [Cambridge: Cambridge University Press, 1939]), who remains, in my estimation, its greatest theorist. For a useful review, see Leo Kuper and M.G. Smith, eds., _Pluralism in Africa_ (Berkeley: University of California Press, 1971).

[10] _The Concept of Law_ (Oxford: The Clarendon Press, 1961), pp. 26-48.

as customs, which confer powers on private individuals (e.g., to make wills and contracts) are seen as anomalies. The pluralists also take issue with the view of a sovereign unrestrained by further laws or "secondary rules," as Hart would call them. The command theory of the state seems to discount the ideas of constitutionalism and the rule of law--seems to overlook the extent to which the concepts of "rules" and "orders" diverge. On this point, the criticism of Hayek is particularly apt:

> In observing such [general] rules, we do not serve another person's end, nor can we properly be said to be subject to his will. My action can hardly be regarded as subject to the will of another person if I use his rules for my own purposes as I might use my knowledge of a law of nature, and if that person does not know of my existence or of the particular circumstances in which the rules will apply to me or of the effects they will have on my plans.[11]

The command theory seems also to discount the extent to which the state is a partnership between private associations with specific interests and concerns and public institutions with general responsibilities, and the extent to which the cooperation and good will of the former is essential for legislation to be legitimate and effective.

The political theory of pluralism contains two further concepts of importance to this study: (1) the conception of society as constituted of a large number of voluntary associations, and (2) the related conception of a clear boundary marking off society from the state--the "private" from the "public" realm. Society tends to be the purposive, active realm; government, the responsible and reactive realm. But reactions in the forms of adjustments in public policies (for example) are believed capable of eliciting further actions by groups in society. Hence it is possible for Ernest Barker to speak of "the parallel growth of Society and the State, of voluntary co-operation and political regulation."[12] The benefits of such a "plural state" are believed to reside both in the opportunities it provides for the flourishing of voluntary group action (and the general social benefits of such action) and in the possibilities it creates for enhanced political rationality resulting from the responsive adjustment of public policies to

---

[11]Friedrich A. Hayek, The Constitution of Liberty (Chicago: University of Chicago Press, 1960), pp. 152-53.

[12]Principles of Social and Political Theory (New York: Oxford University Press, 1961), p. 50.

the interests and concerns of affected groups in society. In
the plural polity, society and state are regarded as mutually
dependent spheres.

The sociological theory of non-Western pluralism is
quite different from the political theory of Western pluralism.
It begins not with a theory of the state but with a concept of
society--the "plural society." Paradoxically, the plural society
is not a society at all, if by that term is meant what Webster
defines as either "an enduring and cooperating social group whose
members have developed organized patterns of relationships
through interaction with one another" or "a community, nation
or broad grouping of people having common traditions, institutions, and collective activities and interests." It is rather
a medley of stateless societies: an assemblage of contiguous,
closed communities in which membership is ascriptive and
mandatory. This image contrasts sharply with the concept of
society in Western pluralism as a system of open, voluntary
associations--essentially the definition of Barker:

> By "Society" we mean the whole sum of voluntary bodies,
> or associations. . . . These associations form the social
> substance which goes by the general and comprehensive name
> of "Society."[13]

In this conception, multiple overlapping memberships are regarded
as both possible and desirable, since associations are open; in
the plural society conception, this is impossible, since each
constituent community is a closed group--a kind of proto-state.

For Furnivall, who coined the term, a "plural society"
is "a society comprising two or more [cultural] elements or
social orders which live side by side, yet without mingling,
in one political unit."[14] This definition underlines the importance of the state: the plural assemblage of closed communities is rendered a "society" only by encapsulation within a
common political unit. For Furnivall that unit was the colonial
state. The power (rather than the "authority") of that state
was essential for holding the colonial society together, especially during periods of awakened national consciousness when communities came into conflict:

> Nationalism sets one community against the other so as to
> emphasize the plural character of the society and aggravate

---

[13] Barker, p. 3.

[14] Furnivall, p. 446.

its instability, thereby enhancing the need for it to be held together by some force exerted from outside.[15]

In the hands of later sociological writers, coercive rule by a single community--typically an alien minority--takes the place of the colonial state. The emphasis is upon communal coercion and conflict. Summing up this sociological view, van den Berghe observes that

> conflict theorists came to the conclusion that pluralism is associated with despotic minority rule and with relative lack of consensus on both values legitimizing the existing polity and norms regulating political behavior.[16]

These two theories imply radically different types of polities. The first theory implies a plural polity of active and specialized open associations--"voluntary in origin," "specific in purpose"[17]--that are free and, presumably, competent to register an interest or concern in legislation and public policy. Their typical indifference to policy unrelated to their interests or concerns can be interpreted as evidence of civility, although David Truman has used the apparent fact of "overlapping memberships" to account for the indifference.[18] Implied is a kind of "market" politics of discussion and compromise involving "bargaining," "negotiation," "consultation," and general good will in spite of policy partisanship: a system of "partisan mutual adjustment," as Charles Lindblom would say.[19] Applied without revision to contemporary underdeveloped countries--either by attributing the characteristics of interest groups to communal groups, or by suggesting that a quick process of "associational development" is required to overcome the deficiencies of the

---

[15] Ibid., p. 459.

[16] Pierre L. van den Berghe, "Pluralism and the Polity: A Theoretical Exploration" in Kuper and Smith, eds., p. 73.

[17] Barker, p. 3.

[18] David B. Truman, The Governmental Process (New York: Alfred A. Knopf, 1951). Mancur Olson disputes the assertion of widespread overlapping memberships in the United States (The Logic of Collective Action [Cambridge, Mass.: Harvard University Press, 1965]).

[19] Charles E. Lindblom, The Intelligence of Democracy (New York: The Free Press, 1965), and The Policy-Making Process (Englewood Cliffs: Prentice-Hall, 1968).

non-Western society--the political theory stands in danger of misconceiving non-Western pluralism and its communal norms.

The sociological theory discounts the possibility of political pluralism in the non-Western plural society, which is conceived to be plural only in a special sociological sense. And its social pluralism is conceived in such a way that, in its present form, only coercive minority rule can contain the centrifugal pressures caused by communal differences. Because the plural society is segmented into more or less self-contained communal groups with their own distinctive norms and values, there is no institutional basis for the operation of a general, pan-communal system of legitimate government. Applied without revision to the post-colonial underdeveloped countries, the sociological theory leads us to conclude that these countries either must be ruled coercively or their societies must be changed--presumably by some process of successful "nation-building," so that a consensus on basic political values and norms can be established.

Thus both these theories--the political and the sociological--lead to the inescapable conclusion that underdeveloped countries either must be governed coercively (that is, without the consideration of existing political norms) or they must be transformed or "developed" into a system that has usable norms. Both theories overlook the possibility that the non-Western plural society may contain the social foundations of a different kind of "communal polity"--a polity resting on an undeclared social constitution of communal norms that encourages the alternative development of a system of personal rule based largely on the institution of patronage.

The Communal Group

A political theory of non-Western pluralism must begin by revising the familiar distinction between the "private" and the "public" because the plural society will confound any analysis that proceeds from this distinction. In the communal polity, neither "society" nor the "state" is quite what we ordinarily assume it to be--nor (as we shall see later) is "government" quite what we assume it to be.

The key political unit of a communal polity--the communal group--is best conceived not as a private interest but rather as a kind of para-public, a proto-state within a state. The para-public nature of the communal group can be seen in an analysis of both its internal and external political characteristics. Internally, the "publicness" of a communal group is indicated by its affording its members a more or less complete or rounded and culturally distinctive way of life. The group's way of life is culturally distinctive by reason of its unique language, customs, religion, economic practices, and so on, which--separately or in combination--provide members with a common sense of their unique identity. Such characteristics are public characteristics: they are external or public signs borne by all members. (The fact that they must be concealed or disavowed by any members who do not wish to belong to the community or who would prefer to belong to another community is an indication of the "publicness" of such characteristics.) Because it provides members with a culturally distinctive way of life, the communal group is the natural locus for the evolution of common rules, of common rights and duties, of a prescribed system of communal norms. Such norms suggest the idea of the "communal good" which can be appealed to over the narrower and more parochial interests of factions or individuals within the community. To conceive of such a common appeal is to conceive of the communal group as some kind of political unit or public.

Communal groups typically comprise smaller units. For instance, "tribal" groups often comprise smaller descent groups (clans, extended families), strata based upon some scale of social prestige (such as political rank, age, material possessions), and particular spatial units (such as regions, locations, or settlements). And groups that might qualify for the label "ethnic" often can be divided internally in various and manifold ways.[20] If the internal life of communities typically is marked by divisions such as these, we must make conceptual allowance for the possibility that the cosmopolitan communal public may evaporate in the face of internal conflicts among members and factions. From the perspective of political theory, the point is not that communal groups are always solid, united blocs--for surely they are not[21]--but that when they function as united groups within the jurisdictional orbit of the larger, new state, they are likely to function more as publics than as ordinary interest groups. And modernization, far from dissolving the communal public, often tends to promote it. By fostering social insecurity and uncertainty, such forces as the market economy or urbanization are likely to encourage mutual aid based on the prescriptive rules of communal fellowship. What were quite informal conventions of kinship obligation in the rural regions of new states often become more precisely delineated

---

[20]Nathan Glazer and Daniel Moynihan, eds., Ethnicity: Theory and Experience (Cambridge, Mass.: Harvard University Press, 1975).

[21]Fredrik Barth, ed., Ethnic Groups and Boundaries (Boston: Little, Brown, 1969).

rules of mutual assistance and ethnic association in the urban areas.[22]

The para-public nature of a communal group can be seen also in its external affairs and in the boundaries it maintains against similar groups within the new state. Unlike interest associations, communal groups ordinarily proscribe the voluntary entrance and exit of members. Being voluntary and open (at least in theory if not always in practice), interest associations facilitate the entrance and exit of members, making membership loyalty the central problem for leaders since dissatisfied members are always in a position to threaten or exercise their option of leaving.[23] Being involuntary and closed, communal groups ordinarily provide no means of entrance or exit save by marriage or, more usually, by birth or death. The latter are of little moment because they mark only the physical but not the spiritual movement of persons into and out of the community-- the communal group reminding one of Burke's "state," i.e., "a partnership not only between those who are living, but between those who are living, those who are dead, and those who are to be born."

Like the "nation," and all other spiritual groups that "possess" their members in this special way, the communal group fosters a conception of "insiders" and "outsiders." Those who cannot claim to belong remain "normative strangers," often even in spite of physical proximity or social intercourse and even in spite of common or shared legal "citizenship." The concept of "normative stranger" or cultural foreigner is a natural vehicle for encouraging ethnocentrism--i.e., a belief in the inherent superiority of one's own membership group and its way of life accompanied by a feeling of contempt for other groups and their ways of living. By restricting entrance and exit, and hence preventing the development of multiple, moderate identities of the sort that tend to characterize a modern plural polity, the communal group--like the nation but unlike the voluntary association--serves as a closed arena for the encourage- ment of such ethnocentrism. Community boundaries may thereby constitute serious obstacles to the establishment of national citizenship rules, which must be indifferent to communalism. In the international system, such obstacles have their counter- part in the national barriers that stand in the way of attempts to establish global moral rules according to which the citizens

---

[22]William Hanna and Judith Hanna, eds., Urban Dynamics in Black Africa (Chicago: Aldine-Atherton, 1971).

[23]A.O. Hirschman, Voice, Exit and Loyalty (Cambridge, Mass.: Harvard University Press, 1970), pp. 76-105.

of one country would have the duty to extend aid to and the right to receive aid from the citizens of other countries.[24]

An analysis of the para-public properties of the communal group requires a conceptualization of the "communal interest" that would enable us to distinguish it from other kinds of interests--for instance, associational group interests or the national interest. The problem of defining "interests" in political theory is not a simple one,[25] but a workable conception for our purposes may be approached by observing that the statement "x is in A's interest" is something like saying "A wants x" or "A will be satisfied with x." This is the approach of John Plamenatz, who by one definition calls an interest ' "whatever is profitable to a person or group, because it gives him or them what he or they want or will find satisfactory."[26] This definition does not address the question whether individual and group profit (or satisfaction) must always be identical. It is, of course, doubtful that they ever will be identical, but a group theory that operated on any other assumption would be quite at sea, and so it is necessary to find reasons for assuming this or something very nearly like it. In the case of voluntary associations, the opportunity of exit is one reason for assuming that the interest of the group must conform fairly well to that of its members.[27] A second reason for assuming a basic identity of interests between group and members is the fact that most associations have specialized interests or concerns, and that their members are drawn together by these special interests. Like-minded persons of similar backgrounds are usually drawn into similar association. Finally--and most important--it is characteristic of most associations to be organized and led by a member or minority responsible to the group and, to some extent, for the group. Hence, it is not unreasonable to conceive a group interest to be whatever its leaders or fiduciaries declare it to be. Typically, we assume the presence of a specialized interest or concern on the part of an interest group, and we ascertain it by asking group leaders or fiduciaries (more than ordinary members) what it is.

---

[24]Peter Singer, "Famine, Affluence and Morality," Philosophy and Public Affairs, Vol. 1 (Spring 1972), pp. 229-43.

[25]For some recent attempts at definition, see the symposium on "interest" in Political Theory, Vol. 3 (August 1975), pp. 245-88.

[26]John P. Plamenatz, "Interest (Political Science)" in Julius Gould and William Kolb, eds., A Dictionary of the Social Sciences (New York: The Free Press, 1964), p. 343.

[27]Hirschman.

I have smuggled the word "concern" into the analysis
because the concept of "interest" is too restrictive for a group
theory of politics. Having a concern in something suggests
something more general and social than merely having an interest
in it. Brian Barry has distinguished "interest groups" from
"cause groups"--the latter organized not so much to satisfy
private wants as to promote social causes.[28] And Lindblom has
remarked how

> many groups pursue versions of the "public interest.". . .
> Many other groups pursue specific narrow interests, but
> not the interests of the members. . . . As E.E. Schatt-
> schneider has said, the members of the American League to
> Abolish Capital Punishment obviously do not expect to be
> hanged.[29]

Thus there are times and places when we want to speak of groups
with causes and concerns, and to distinguish such groups from
those with merely interests.

Political theory is interested in groups only insofar
as their interests, concerns, or causes are in some way "political"--that is, only insofar as they relate in some way to the
common affairs of the society or to the interests, concerns,
or causes of other groups or sectors of society. Typically,
interests, concerns, or causes are considered political when
they are attentive to government laws, policies, and activities.
Conceptually, interests or concerns are relational: we ordinarily
speak of having an interest in, or a concern about, something
or someone. When we are speaking of political interests and
concerns, that something or someone usually is a government
policy or action.[30] We can think in terms of an interest-concern
and policy-law nexus. To know the political interests of a
trade union, say, we would ask its leaders or spokesmen (rather
than some average members) whether a specific government regulation or even a more general law or policy was agreeable to them.
By implication, a policy will be agreeable to the extent that,
in the leaders' judgment, it places the members in a better
position to satisfy their wants, or in a period of austerity, to
the extent that it does not place them in a worse position.

If it makes sense to think of group interests or concerns
as important determinants of public policies, it makes equal

---

[28]*Political Argument* (London: Routledge & Kegan Paul, 1965),
pp. 64-65.

[29]Lindblom, p. 63.

[30]Barry, p. 174.

sense to think of laws and policies as arousing and focusing the political interests and concerns of groups. If interest group leaders evaluate policies in terms of the advantages or disadvantages--relative to some other policy or to some other group--to their membership, the leaders of cause groups evaluate policies more in terms of their conformity with the ideals that their members espouse. It is considered likely--and much has been made of this point by many political sociologists--that the interests or concerns of groups will reflect the common socio-economic circumstances (class position, income, occupation, education, and so on) of their members. But I believe it is just as likely that such interests and concerns will reflect the common impact of public laws and policies on the members. The relationship between political interests (and concerns) and public laws and policies is a reciprocal one.

I have been talking of the political interests and concerns characteristic of a modern, plural polity whose social structure is differentiated along associational group lines. But the argument can also be applied to class-stratified societies in which class interests and ideologies are given political expression. One can speak easily of a class interest or class ideology and public laws-and-policies nexus--both class interests and ideologies being capable of affecting the acts of modern government and of being affected by government. This is particularly the case with respect to laws and policies that raise the issue of equality--i.e., of class advantage or disadvantage relative to other classes in society or relative to some standard of opportunity or welfare. Indeed, the modern conception of justice is closely keyed to the ideal of equality and, through that ideal, to the presence of classes and the fact of class inequality.

It is much more difficult to speak of the interests or concerns of communal groups in this way. For reasons having to do with the categorically different characteristics of "policies" and "communal groups," it is difficult to speak of a communal interest in specific public policies. For one thing, the modern conception of legislation and public policy rests upon the ideal of legal generality and impartiality operating within the domain of the national society. This ideal precludes official discrimination, in relation to either persons or groups of persons, on any basis having to do with the ascribed characteristics of such persons or groups. The establishmentof this ideal in modern states is a victory won, in some places and with respect to some groups, only in the last few decades--a victory of a liberal ideal.[31] Thus, in the United States today, "reverse" or

---

[31]Nathan Glazer, _Affirmative Discrimination: Ethnic Inequality and Public Policy_ (New York: Basic Books, 1975).

"compensatory" discrimination (such as the preferential hiring
of women or members of minority groups) is usually thought to
require a justification beyond the linguistic sleight of
designating "sex" or "ethnicity" as a qualification.[32] The
same universal standard precludes the enactment of special laws
or public policies which regulate the activities of (or extend
benefits to) a particular category of persons deliberately
defined so as to exclude other similarly qualified persons who
do not belong to that category. Thus we ordinarily would speak
of "federal" urban policy (applied impartially to all urban
areas defined in accordance with a general rule), but not of
"Boston" policy, "New York City" policy, "San Francisco" policy,
etc., except where these were components of a general policy.

Except for a few special policy areas, modern legislation and policies ordinarily cannot be formulated, enacted, and
implemented with only particular communal groups in view. Modern
policy domains are open domains accessible by qualification
rather than ascription. This means that it would be unlikely
that all persons who qualified for a policy (or were interested
in it) would be members of a specific communal group. Even a
policy on communalism would, under the rule of legal generality,
have to apply without prejudice to all communities rather than
any particular one(s). Otherwise the policy would be discriminatory, and could be spoken of as a "policy" only by distorting
the usual meaning of the word. Modern governments usually are
organized into specialized ministries, departments, or agencies
responsible for implementing and enforcing policies in congruent
and similarly specialized domains of society. In public administration we can conceive of "generalists" and "experts" or
"specialists," but not of "particularists." The domains of
policy and law ideally are open categories of citizens whose
actions or attainments qualify them to belong: income categories,
age categories, occupational categories, property ownership
categories, welfare categories, and so on. Such "artificial"
domains are likely to cut across the closed, cultural boundaries
of communal groups, making it problematic both for the communal
interest to be an interest in policy and for policies to be
targeted exclusively at such communities.

How, therefore, should we conceive of the communal
interest? Since communal groups appear to resemble nations
more than interest groups, it would seem sensible to approach a
definition of the communal interest by using the analogy of the

---

[32]Thomas Nagel, "Equal Treatment and Compensatory Discrimination," Philosophy and Public Affairs, Vol. 2 (Summer 1973),
pp. 348-63; Judith Thomson, "Preferential Hiring," ibid., pp.
364-84.

national interest. Barry defines the "national interest" as
the interests that inhabitants of one country share in their
country's international relations with other countries.[33] By
analogy, we could define the "communal interest" as the shared
interests of members of one community in its external relations
with other communities. But the use of the analogy is limited
because the communal interest is externally oriented not only
toward other communal interests in the plural society, but also
toward the national government. We already have seen how communal groups ordinarily cannot make a claim for restrictive
legislation or policies that would exclude members of other
communities who would otherwise qualify. Ordinarily they cannot
be a domain of public policy or declare an interest in substantive
policies. What, then, is the substance of their collective
interests and concerns? It is, I shall argue, the protection
of their public property: their culture and way of life.

In a modern state, distinctive subcultures ordinarily
are not workable or legitimate domains of public policy, and
historically they have not been recognized as such by modern
national governments. Being the distinctive public property
of communities, cultural lifeways based on religion or language,
for instance, are usually thought to be too important to be
attended to by public policies--even if those policies can be
made consistent with the requirement of legal generality. It
is true that legislation has been used to provide security for
communal cultures--typically by establishment of a statutory
agency for that purpose. Ministries of language, education,
or cultural affairs sometimes attend to such matters, or--where
the communities can be defined territorially--they may be handled
by ministries of local government. But these methods usually
are not thought to provide enough security.

In the historical experience of the modern, European-type
state, subcultural concerns like religion or language usually
have been treated as civil "rights," and have been protected
under special rules and authorities instituted for that purpose.
In the legal and political theory of the modern state, such subcultures typically are conceived as special "public" domains
within the state requiring a constitutional guarantee or safeguard of some kind. Sometimes these guarantees have been provided
through schemes of divided constitutional jurisdiction--for instance, by some system of federalism. This "federal" solution
acknowledges the "public" nature of the subcultural domains by
extending the right of self-government in specified spheres to
them. By these methods, the subcultural para-public interest is
made a legitimate and integral part of the general, public interest.

---

[33] Barry, p. 203.

Upon the achievement of independence by most new states--
certainly most former British colonies--constitutional methods of
accommodating communal interests were tried.[34]   But very few of
these institutional experiments were successful. In particular,
the frequent failure of constitutional experiments with federal-
ism--failures registered most often in civilian coups by dominant
political parties, or in military coups--might be taken as an indication that the communal interests have been overridden or suppressed in those countries where such coups have taken place. No
doubt many civilian or military usurpers, in their desire to con-
solidate power, have wished that this were so, and perhaps some
have tried to make it so. But the pervasiveness of the plural
society and its norms, coupled with the generally limited scope
and effectiveness of the powers of the new autocrats, has made it
difficult for communal interests to be suppressed. A monopoly of
coercive power might permit the usurpers to rule autocratically,
but coercion alone cannot eliminate the deeply and widely felt
sentiments and loyalties that attach to communal groups, or guarantee that these sentiments will not influence the actions of
state agents. Repeated complaints, in military and civilian regimes alike, against "communalism," "tribalism," "nepotism,"
"patronage," and "corruption" suggest quite the opposite. Indeed,
they suggest that once extra-legal political methods are resorted
to by one significant political group to capture and hold power
in the state, they will be resorted to by all other groups that
wish to influence that power.[35]   A regime of extra-legal influence
hardly seems to preclude the possibility for communal interests
and concerns to be registered and attended to within the state.
Thus legislation and constitutional engineering are not the only
political methods for protecting or advancing the interests and
concerns of communal groups: they are only the most distinctively
modern methods.

There is another modern method that belongs, conceptually,
to a regime of policy government, but can nevertheless promote
the interests and concerns of communal groups. It is related
to a particular category of government decision-making--i.e.,
decisions that pertain to the siting of (usually) large and
expensive public projects, such as highways, railways, harbors,

---

[34]Some interesting discussions of applied political theory, now
sadly neglected, attended these attempts--at least those by the
British; see Hansard Society, Problems of Parliamentary Government in Colonies, and What Are the Problems of Parliamentary
Government in West Africa? (London: Hansard Society, 1953 and
1958), and Kenneth Kirkwood, ed., African Affairs, Number 10
(London: Chatto & Windus, 1961).

[35]Samuel Huntington, Political Order in Changing Societies
(New Haven: Yale University Press, 1968).

dams, irrigation schemes, and so on. The modern method of making such policy decisions involves the impartial application of technical-economic criteria to determine the relative qualifications of different possible sites. In societies where government is actively involved in the making of many such decisions--e.g., in mixed economies where the state ordinarily is engaged in the provision of economic infrastructure and (of course) in socialist societies--it is likely that considerations of distributive justice will be added to the technical-economic criteria, resulting typically in "trade-offs" between productivity and equality.

When such criteria effectively govern the siting of large public projects, the decision-making procedures are consistent with the modern ideal of policy government, but their effects in a plural society may not be what is most desirable. Such decisions ordinarily result in the allocation of benefits to particular geographic sites and therefore to the particular groups occupying the sites rather than to the categories of persons who may best qualify for them. The domains of such decisions may be congruent with the boundaries of territorially based communal groups. It is quite conceivable, therefore, that such decisions would appeal to the collective interests and concerns of such groups. Indeed, there is little doubt that the communal interest in these kinds of allocative decisions is intense in most contemporary plural societies. In pluralist Nigeria, for instance, the political and governmental process has been characterized as little more than the intensive rivalry of regional-communal groups to participate in "sharing the national cake."[36] Here we come to one of those political paradoxes of public-minded statism that lead to sectional and para-public-minded communalism in underdeveloped countries. The more that governments in underdeveloped plural societies have wanted to become directly engaged in the making of such allocative decisions, have wanted to pursue an economic development strategy of public planning and state intervention in such matters, have wanted (presumably) to apply the modern norms of policy government, the more they have unintentionally invited a politics of communal rivalry which would dispense with modern standards of productivity and equality. Since such allocative decisions tend to be one-of-a-kind decisions, it is easy for each to be perceived as of special importance, and for particularistic, non-policy criteria to intrude still further into the decision-making process. The congruence of the domains of such allocative decisions with communal group boundaries, coupled with the uniqueness of individual projects, is likely to result

---

[36] Ojetunji Aboyade, "Relations Between Central and Local Institutions in the Development Process" in Arnold Rivkin, ed., Nations by Design (New York: Anchor Books, 1968), p. 101.

finally in the substitution of patronage norms for those of
policy, as it has in otherwise "modern" polities like the United
States.

Here then is a modern, public-minded type of government
decision-making where a prima facie argument can be made for
the compatibility of policymaking and the communal interest, but
where further analysis reveals reasons for believing that the
policy norms for making such decisions will be displaced by
alternative norms of political patronage. Even in countries with
a strong sense of the public interest, such decisions can invite
patronage norms--the case, for instance, in the U.S. national
highways program. In underdeveloped countries, where the general
public is dimly perceived and where the para-public communal
group is a force to be reckoned with, it should hardly be sur-
prising that the concepts and vocabulary of patronage seem most
apt for describing the allocative process. (This line of
argument will be developed further in Chapters III and IV below.)

The Communal Polity

In pluralist political theory we have seen how "public"
and "private" approximate the distinction between state and
society--or between government agencies and their regulatory
authority, on the one hand, and voluntary associations and their
influence, on the other. These distinctions presuppose the
very important concept of a normative boundary separating state
and society, public agents and private interests.

In theory, pluralism is destroyed if this boundary is
obliterated--if the equilibrium between the public and the
private spheres is upset, leading to domination by one sphere.
This can happen in one of two opposite ways: either by the
"nationalization" of the private realm and the consequent aboli-
tion of voluntary associations and interest groups, or by the
domination of public agencies and officials by powerful private
interests. In pluralist thought, the first method is generally
associated with the proliferation of public agencies and often
with statism and socialism, the second method with the domination
of the state by powerful and assertive private groups. The
integrity of the public/private boundary is a dominant normative
concern not only of modern pluralist thought, but of general
political discussion as well. Whether employed as a conceptual
tool or as a political standard, it has simplified the task of
analyzing and justifying (or condemning) the acts of both government and private agents. It has thereby provided the foundation for a normative theory of modern government.

But perhaps it has allowed us to forget the earlier,
more complicated and less universalistic theory it replaced, and

103020

the more varied and diverse ways that the "public" and "private" boundary could be drawn and could be confused in pre-modern, European society. Even the briefest glance back at the underlying theory of pre-modern European government reveals something of this conceptual complexity and, by way of contrast, something of the extent to which the modern public/private distinction has had a simplifying effect upon political thought and practice. Such a backward glance reveals a more complex and less standardized type of pluralism in which "government" cannot so readily be conceived as an impersonal public agency. Its "offices" often were not public in the sense of being publicly owned and accountable; indeed, sometimes they were the privately appropriated property of the members of a privileged political class. The concept of the separation of private and public property, of personal and impersonal administration, was not fully incorporated into the theory and practice of European government until the eighteenth or nineteenth centuries. This certainly was the case with regard to British administration, where civil service reform came quite late,[37] but also with regard to continental European governments.[38]

The pluralism of pre-modern and early modern European society is, for the greater part, a legalistic patchwork of various kinds of social strata, collectivities, and corporate bodies--estates, churches, guilds, companies, municipalities, universities, and so on--many with their own internal system of ranks, orders, and statuses, and each with its own sphere of common or "public" affairs, often defined in law. Municipal corporations, trade-guilds, or chartered companies, for example, typically operated under legal patents or licenses (granted by a ruler) which provided their officials with the authority to regulate the public life of the collectivity. In such a legalistically plural society within which numerous semi-autonomous collectivities carried on their own "public" affairs relatively free from outside intrusion, it was difficult to speak of the general public or the public-at-large. The "political nation" could be spoken of (and in England was spoken of as recently as the eighteenth century) as the assembled representatives of the political class.[39] In England it also was possible to speak of

---

[37] Henry Parris, Constitutional Bureaucracy (London: George Allen & Unwin, 1969), pp. 21-80.

[38] Eugene Anderson and Pauline Anderson, Political Institutions and Social Change in Continental Europe in the Nineteenth Century (Berkeley: University of California Press, 1967), pp. 166-237.

[39] Parris.

lesser "nations":   "You are a subtle nation, you physicians."[40]
The compelling and often romantic abstraction of the modern
"nation" arose as a political concept of a general, "national"
populace only in the eighteenth and nineteenth centuries.[41]

A greatly simplified model of such a polity might help
us to distinguish the characteristics of its dual public and
private domains. These distinctions can be represented graphical-
ly by the intersection of two conceptually different public/
private boundaries:

Public I	Private I
Public II	Private II

Such a polity can be conceived to be divided (or "politically stratified") vertically between (1) a very narrow ruling
class of privileged persons, comprised typically of landed
aristocrats and the sovereign, whose political status and house-
holds/estates constitute the Public I, the character of which is
suggested by such terms as "realm," "state," or "political
nation";** and (2) the assembled collectivities arranged at
various levels below the ruling class whose particular (often
local) autonomies, rights, and powers constitute a dispersed
Public II, the character of which is suggested by such terms as
"estates," "corporations," "municipal corporations," and the
like, which imply non-state jurisdiction. Such a higher public/
lower public distinction, as Barker observes,

> belongs to a graded and hierarchical society, in which
> there are different states or "Estates" (or sorts and con-
> ditions of men) arranged in ascending degrees, and one of
> these states or "Estates" is the State par excellence.
> [Emphasis in original.][42]

In pre-industrial England, according to Laslett, the vertical
class division was reflected in the system of ranks and orders
that separated the gentry or political grades from the

---

[40]K.R. Minogue, Nationalism (Baltimore: Penguin Books, 1970),
p. 9.

[41]Williams, pp. 178-80.

**When the political class was not "loyal" to its sovereign,
the "political nation" could easily dissolve into warring
parties or factions or even into armed political camps, as hap-
pened during the English civil war.

[42]Barker, p. 91.

nonpolitical, ordinary grades below.[43] This division--and particularly the exclusive privileges of the Public I--received the greatest degree of critical attention in modern democratic thought, and ultimately disappeared through democratic revolution or reform in many European countries. Distinctions of political rank were destroyed by replacing a restrictive system of rights and duties with a universal system based on the concept of equal citizenship. But the democratic revolution left largely untouched those differences of power and influence that derived from differences in social status and private wealth: it was more a revolution of rights than of powers.

Related changes in political theory and practice affecting the horizontal public/private divisions of the pre-modern European type of polity are worth noting. Two general developments are of particular interest. First, revised legal ideas and reforms had the effect of removing or transforming many of the exclusive rights exercised by semi-autonomous, non-state jurisdictions (Public II), resulting both in the subordination of such jurisdictions to Public I and in a proliferation of private associations and contractual relations (Private II) operating within the jurisdiction of Public I. A corporative society (Public II) was eventually transformed into a contractual society (Private II) of freely associating individuals and groups. Second, a revised concept of "public" government and administration was formulated which led eventually to major changes or reforms in the rules and practices pertaining to the occupation of political and administrative office. More than ever in the past, government was conceived as the representative of the citizenry--of the greatly enlarged general public. To implement this conception, new rules and regulations were devised concerning the election (less often the selection) of representatives and governments which typically were national in character. The administrative branch was conceived as the agent of government and the servant of the general public. Rules and regulations based upon the concept of "merit" were formulated and applied to administrative appointments and promotions; merit and impartiality replaced patronage and favoritism--at least in theory, if not always in practice. In England, for instance, an uncentralized and makeshift administration staffed largely by royal and parliamentary patronage was reformed into a permanent, centrally organized "civil service" staffed (ideally) by merit appointees.[44] Here as elsewhere the development of a modern public bureaucracy involved the strict separation of the

---

[43]Peter Laslett, The World We Have Lost (New York: Charles Scribner's Sons, 1965), p. 38.

[44]Parris, pp. 21-79.

administrative office from its particular incumbent--the Public I from the Private I.[45]

Such changes resulted in the establishment of a kind of polity that can be analyzed and evaluated by the political theory of pluralism discussed earlier--i.e., a polity conceived as comprising a general Public I of all citizens who collectively form that compulsory legal association called the "state," and also comprising a free and open society (Private II) of the same individuals organized into manifold voluntary associations and groups, many of which have interests in public policies but not the authority to make policy. No longer the "owners" of the state apparatus, the rulers are transformed into a government of representatives (elected politicians) and their agents (civil servants) responsible to the ruled, who have been transformed into a citizenry of universally enfranchised adults. No longer political outsiders or even subjects, the citizenry become the "general public": the standard "reference group" for enacting and evaluating legislation and public policies.

Recurrent reports of widespread patronage, corruption, factionalism, communalism, and related practices in underdeveloped countries suggest that the great transformation separating state and society, public and private, has yet to take place. To the extent that such practices are socially acceptable and consistent with valid norms, we are on dubious grounds if we assume that there is a distinct boundary separating the new states from the old societies where such practices are widespread. Indeed, the commonplace character and normatively valid practice of patronage and corruption in such countries implies that the modern norms that uphold the distinction between state and society, public and private, are invalid there. Conceived in this way, such practices call into question any theory of government in underdeveloped countries as an agency responsible to the general public and charged with deliberating upon, making, and enforcing public decisions. They recall, rather, that older conception of parliament that Burke spoke of disparagingly as "a congress of ambassadors from different and hostile interests" which he wanted to contrast with its modern counterpart:

> [A] deliberative assembly of one nation with one interest, that of the whole--where not local prejudices ought to guide but the general good resulting from the general reason of the whole.[46]

---

[45]Bendix and Roth, eds., p. 130.

[46]Harvey C. Mansfield, Jr., "Rationality and Representation in Burke's 'Bristol Speech'" in Carl Friedrich, ed., Nomos VII: Rational Decision (New York: Atherton, 1967), p. 205.

THE COMMUNAL POLITY

In the language of this study, pre-modern politics within a
state can be conceived to be more like a struggle among communal
groups and their representatives to possess the means of government for their own enjoyment than a contest among groups to
influence legislation and policies in an effort to satisfy the
interests or concerns of their members. In such a conception,
government is not so much a rational instrument for determining
and implementing policies as an edifice whose offices can be
appropriated by the representatives of communal groups: government becomes an object of political annexation and occupation
rather than a target of policy demands.

On this analysis we cannot conceive of government as
"publicly owned," but neither (strictly speaking) is it "privately owned." Government authority is not exercised by agents
responsible to the general public and its laws, but neither is
it exercised only in accordance with the personal whim of the
officeholder. It is doubtful that he incurs a duty to the
general public through his appropriation of government office,
but it does not alter his communal obligations and responsibilities. The ineffectiveness of modern institutional rules does
not imply the ineffectiveness of all other norms. Typically
the occupation of an office--by means of patronage, say--will
release an administrative incumbent from the constraints of
official rules and regulations, which is the usual requirement
in modern bureaucratic administration, but he will still have
to justify his actions to his patron or to the community represented by his patron. Even if he is appointed ostensibly by
merit, his obligations to assist friends, relatives, and other
members of his own community will not automatically cease when
he becomes a government official. If anything, they should be
expected to increase since, by occupying an official post, he
now is much better placed to honor them. An East African
cabinet minister recently complained that

in every part of East Africa [following independence], one
[could] witness the undesirable situation in which a member
of a family whose income increases is suddenly and constant-
ly besieged by demands for support from a large number of
distant relatives.[47]

It is highly unlikely that government incumbents could satisfy
such demands (or would be expected to) from their own "private"
resources. It is much more likely that they would use their
"official" position to meet these obligations, and that this
would be expected of them, since under the social constitution

---

[47]Tom Mboya, The Challenge of Nationhood (London: Andre
Deutsch, 1970), p. 174.

PLURALISM

of a communal polity, a refusal could only be conceived as a reprehensible act.

The occupation and annexation of government, of its offices and their assets, by the representatives of communal groups suggests an older idea of government not unlike the one that modern political and administrative reforms made obsolescent in the West. In this conception, government is an edifice of communal representation and patronage rather than a law- and policy-making agency. The reference group that is used to justify this system of government is not the general public, but the communal publics. The norms that are recognized and expected to guide "official" conduct are not the universal ones of the new state but the particular ones of given communities within the plural society. "Government" is not a public, national government so much as a compartmentalized government of subnational publics. Modernization poses a normative dilemma for such a political order, just as it posed such a dilemma for pre-modern European governments: a dilemma of forcing people to choose between different kinds of right and wrong, good and bad, correct and incorrect, proper and improper. If modernization is to succeed, as it has fairly well succeeded in the West, it must change the standards that people ordinarily employ in evaluating the decisions and conduct of public officials and politicians. It must, ultimately, change the minds of people about government and politics.

With these broad conclusions in mind, I now want to probe further into the normative framework of pre-modern, communal government by contrasting its norms with the far more familiar norms of modern public government and its bureaucratic administration.

Chapter III

GOVERNMENT

Policy Government

Our concept of "government"--what it is, what it does,
what it should do--is a modern, positivist concept. Government
is conceived as the business of managing a universitas,[48] as
the impersonal agency of a general public, as a vast and complex
system of purposive organizations authorized to engage in a
multiplicity of public purposes and activities. Government is
the instrument of the state association, the instrument for
attending to the common substantive concerns (or "engagements,"
as Oakeshott would say) of a society: in the modern conception,
a national society, including its regional or local components.
Its goals and activities are guided, ideally and typically, by
public policies: policies that are formulated, implemented,
and evaluated with reference to the general public or some open,
universal category within it. Much public discussion and analysis of modern government pertains to the wisdom or folly of
public policies or the politics and ideals that give rise to
them. We know governments and we approve or disapprove of them
typically by considering their policies.

Modern government, then, is policy government--government
by means of policymaking. This is not to suggest that other
factors, such as personality, cannot enter into our analysis
and evaluation of government actions. People often accept
policies they do not understand solely because their leaders
advocate them, and it is not uncommon for people to vote for
candidates in ignorance or even in disregard of their politics.
But in the modern state it is difficult to make public statements
in support of leaders without commenting upon their politics
and the policies they are likely to lead to. The rational
political man is interested in policies that favor his interests
or ideals; he is interested in personality only insofar as it
has a bearing upon the chances of securing favorable policies.
When the personalities of politicians are criticized, they
typically are criticized only in connection with their politics.
Not only the laws of libel and slander, but also the rules of

---

[48]Michael Oakeshott, On Human Conduct (Oxford: The Clarendon
Press, 1975), pp. 203-206.

fair play make it unacceptable to base political criticsm wholly on the personality or other purely ascribed characteristics of leaders whose policies we oppose.

Policy government is but one conception of government. However, it is a conception that is so familiar to us that we are apt to forget that government has not always sought to operate in accordance with the principles of policymaking. Government can and has operated in accordance with other principles or indeed with no principles--only a blind faith in charismatic leaders. Government actions have been authorized solely by documents (or other tokens) bearing the symbol or "seal" of the ruler. Under this type of "patrimonial" authority (as Max Weber and Reinhard Bendix have stressed), the ruler would want to control the use of his seal, and for that purpose would require some rule or "policy" pertaining to its use once his staff reached a size that was beyond the practical limit of his personal supervision. But this use of the word policy might conceal the extent to which the right to use the seal was "governed" not so much by procedure as by sympathy and mutual understanding between staff and ruler or, where staff members are not personally known to the ruler, by a general sense of personal devotion. In other words, it is a government of patronage and personal loyalty rather than one of policies and procedures. This ideal type of "traditionalist patrimonialism" (as Guenther Roth has pointed out) has some striking conceptual affinities with personal rule in contemporary underdeveloped countries.[49] Its logic is quite consistent with the concept of a personally appropriated and communally annexed government that I have outlined (see esp. pp. 24-26 above). Such a government operates not by formulating and implementing public policies by means of a public bureaucracy, but rather by allowing the representatives of communities to occupy offices and to use considerable personal discretion in exercising authority. To better appreciate the differences between policy government and personal rule, it is necessary to probe further into the modern concepts of "government" and public "policies."

Central to the modern concept of government is the Cartesian ideal of "rationalism"--of an organized activity directed at a public purpose. If "government" generally denotes "the activity or process of governing," of attending to the common affairs of society, then modern government is distinguished by the extent to which it employs legislation, policies, and organization to attend to such affairs. The modern governmental process is disciplined by "policies" that are administered by

[49]"Personal Rulership, Patrimonialism, and Empire-Building" in Bendix and Roth, pp. 156-69.

28

bureaucracies--by a trained officialdom who staff the numerous
and often highly specialized agencies of government. Modern
government is, as Hayek laments, a _taxis_: a teleocratic system
of organizations designed for specific purposes.[50] Planning,
policymaking, and public administration give direction and
discipline to the governmental process, permitting governments
to pursue selected aims. Modern government is not only deliberation (a pre-modern concept), but also activity _guided_ by plans,
programs, procedures, and regulations which are _administered_
by paid public officials, many of whom are experts in special
areas of public policy.

"Policies" are deliberately selected and authorized
courses of action intended to achieve an aim. The _Oxford_
English Dictionary gives the following definition of the political meaning of "policy":

> A course of action adopted and pursued by a government,
> party, ruler, statesman, etc.; any course of action adopted
> as advantageous or expedient.

Indicated here is a notion of policy as chosen means. Similarly,
in _A Dictionary of the Social Sciences_ Wilfred Harrison says
that

> The most common social and political usage of the term
> _policy_ refers to a course of action conceived as deliberate-
> ly adopted, after a review of possible alternatives, and
> pursued, or intended to be pursued.[51]

There is almost inevitably a tension between policies and purposes
in the sense that policies are calculated aims at particular ends
but carry no guarantee of hitting the target. Perhaps this is
why policies can be hotly debated even where a consensus on ends
exists.

Policies characteristically permit or require some actions
while prohibiting others. A policy is a normative concept--a
concept of a rule or procedure that carries the imprimatur of
officiality and authority: "Our policy is . . . ." or "It is
not our policy to . . . ." or "That is not our policy." Policies
can fall far short of the initial hopes invested in them. They

---

[50]Friedrich A. Hayek, _Law, Legislation and Liberty_ (Chicago:
University of Chicago Press, 1973), Vol. 1: _Rules and Order_,
pp. 35-54.

[51]Julius Gould and William Kolb, eds., _A Dictionary of the Social Sciences_ (New York: The Free Press, 1964), p. 509.

can fail to "solve" the problems they were designed to meet or to "realize" the purposes they were intended to serve. They also can invite new problems--typically unanticipated ones. But even when they have patently failed, they can still remain in force: they derive their validity from their authority, not from the problems or purposes they are addressed to. Policies that are not enforced tend to discredit governments, and this is why failed policies often continue to be enforced until they can be changed.

Legislation can certify general aims, but often must delegate the authority to frame the particular policies for pursuing them. Such policies are usually made by administrators rather than legislators. Hayek makes a similar distinction between legislation and administration by conceiving policy to be

> the pursuit by government of the concrete, everchanging aims of the day. It is with the execution of policy in this sense that administration proper is largely concerned.[52]

In this conception, policies are the authorized procedures by which substantive government activities are carried on. Unauthorized activities or the corruption of policies by officials are not policies, although if practiced widely and consistently their effects may be the equivalent of policies. Corruption is a matter of influence and power; policy is a matter of authority. Policies are de jure instructions that "authorize" administrative activities and give direction, sanction, and protection to officials; corruption is a violation of such instructions. Hence it is misleading to speak of corruption as "de facto policy":[53] for logical and linguistic reasons, the words corruption and policy cannot be joined in this way.

Policies are the authorized instruments officials use for pursuing declared public purposes, for "steering" government toward selected aims. We can speak, therefore, of "policy government," which operates by framing, implementing, and enforcing "public policies": the plans, programs, procedures, regulations, etc., that government officials administer. To speak of government as purposive, or to use the metaphor of

---

[52] Hayek, Constitution of Liberty, pp. 214-15.

[53] James C. Scott, Comparative Political Corruption (Englewood Cliffs: Prentice-Hall, 1972), p. 24.

political "steersman,"[54] is really to use a modern, teleocratic
concept. Entailed is the concept of policy as the authoritative
instruments by which governmental rationality is pursued, which
in turn presumes that governments ordinarily have the will and
capability to deal with public or social "problems"--also a
modern idea. All of this entails the further modern notion of
secular, social change. In this connection Richard Titmus
observes that

> the concept [of policy] denotes action about means as well
> as ends and it, therefore, implies change: changing
> situations, systems, practices, behavior. And here we
> should note that the concept of policy is only meaningful
> if we (society, a group, or an organization) believe we
> can effect change in some form or another. We do not have
> policies about the weather because, as yet, we are powerless
> to do anything about the weather.[55]

Once governments begin to conceive of social problems and acquire
the will and capability to deal with them, a modern system of
policy government is born.

Policy government is both analytical and impersonal.
It does not usually attend to the unique circumstances of per-
sons--a typical source of complaint in a policy regime--but to
the common wants, needs, or problems of "categories" of individuals (groups, organizations) and to specified "cases"
within each category. Policies are intended to affect individual
persons or groups only to the extent that their actions, aims,
or circumstances can be identified and classified as belonging
to the domain of a policy, as qualifying for the benefits or
sanctions of a policy. Even those most humanitarian of bureaucrats, social workers, speak the impersonal language of policy
when they refer to their "cases" and "case loads." Neutral
words like "cases," "applicant," "subscriber," "resident,"
which identify persons narrowly as members of analytic categories,
are characteristic of the vocabulary of policy government.
Their effect is to depersonalize and routinize the relations
between bureaucrats and citizens, making those relations conform
as much as possible to the impersonal norm of government-public
relations. Such words may be contrasted with the older, more
personalized words that are characteristic of the contrasting
vocabulary of patronage--for instance, the language of the

---

[54]Karl Deutsch, The Nerves of Government (New York: The Free
Press, 1966).

[55]Richard M. Titmus, Social Policy (New York: Pantheon Books,
1974), pp. 23-24.

professions such as law or medicine. Lawyers speak of their "clients," and often attend to the interests of the whole person by acting, for instance, as fiduciaries or trustees. Doctors in "private" practice who are not yet "specialists" still speak of their "patients," even if the term is losing its original meaning. When medicine becomes bureaucratized and subjected to policy norms, vocabulary reflects the change: a patient becomes a "case" and his illness a special medical "problem" to be treated by a "team" of "specialists."

Public policymaking entails social analysis. The policy-maker relies upon the gathering and analysis of social facts about his policy domain--upon social surveys, commissions of inquiry, routine or special investigations, departmental studies, policy reviews, and a variety of other inquiries conducted either by public officials or by outside "experts." He also relies upon the specialized expertise of professional advisers in the manifold areas of public policy--upon economists, financial advisers, agronomists, scientists, public health experts, psychologists, sociologists, planners, statisticians, and numerous other "experts" whose analyses and counsel are believed to be crucial to the rational formulation and implementation of public policy. The impersonal, analytical character of many of these "policy sciences" is revealed particularly by their tendency to categorize and classify social phenomena or problems in order to analyze them. The abstract character of modern public accounting developed in connection with the growth of the taxation authority of government is particularly characteristic of the impersonal and analytical characteristics of policy government. So is statistics, which may be the abstract "policy science" par excellence, the development of which has made social accounting a capability of modern government. Once government became concerned with the general welfare and with "social problems" in the conviction that it could ameliorate them, the need for reliable social statistics arose. The intimate connection between the development of statistics and the concept of social welfare is revealed in the nineteenth-century constitution of the Statistical Society of London, which was established to gather, analyze, and publish "Facts calculated to illustrate the Condition and Prospects of Society."[56] Henceforth the methods of statistics became a characteristic of policy government.

Policies analyze and classify the world. What H.L.A. Hart has said of law can also be said of policy:

---

[56]Philip Abrams, The Origins of British Sociology, 1834-1914 (Chicago: University of Chicago Press, 1968), pp. 14-15.

32

[T]he law must predominantly . . . refer to <u>classes</u> of acts,
things, and circumstances; and its successful operation
over vast areas of social life depends on a widely diffused
capacity to recognize particular acts, things and circumstances as instances of the general classifications which
the law makes.[57]

Policies provide officials with authorized instructions to
regulate types of activities, to respond to types of problems,
to distribute types of benefits, and generally to intervene in
identifiable and pre-selected realms of social life. In the
modern state there are policies for the aged, youth, parents,
children, the sick, the infirm, wage-earners, investors, employers,
employees, the unemployed, homeowners, tenants, landlords, auto-
mobile drivers, transportation operators, passengers, proprietors,
customers. . . . The list is virtually endless: as diversified
as modern society itself.

It is perhaps an exaggeration (but only slightly so) to
say that modern policy government creates and enhances societal
diversity--an effect that is remarkable only for being given
such relatively little notice by modern political analysis.
Within contemporary political science, the view that government
decisions and policies are essentially responses to political
demands and support, including the demands and support of
interest and cause groups, is widely held.[58] I think that this
conception would be closer to the actual process of modern policy
government if allowance were made for the possibility that prior
policies could activate the interests or concerns of groups.
Samuel Beer has observed that the modern, public policymaking
process tends to be purposive and "creative,"[59] and Lindblom
has underlined the fact that governmental policymaking "manu-
factures both policies <u>and</u> preferences."[60] We should conceive
of policy government creating or, rather, inspiring politics
just as we conceive of political interests making demands for
policies. And we should conceive of policies as actions of
modern government which "politicize" society in a way that makes
it possible and rational for individuals equally affected by

---

[57]Hart, p. 121.

[58]David Easton, <u>A Framework for Political Analysis</u> (Englewood
Cliffs: Prentice-Hall, 1965), and <u>A Systems Analysis of Political
Life</u> (New York: Wiley, 1965).

[59]<u>Modern Political Development</u> (New York: Random House, 1974),
pp. 20-22.

[60]Lindblom, <u>Policy-Making Process</u>, p. 102.

the policies to have a reason for uniting in political action. In this sense, policies can "galvanize" and hence "collectivize" individuals into group politics: policies thus produce politics just as they are produced by politics.

In a regime of policy government, politics is a contest to influence and control the policymaking process. The point of modern political action is to secure desirable policies--policies that are in line with an individual's or a group's ideals or interests. It goes without saying that benefits of a personal, noncollective nature--non-policy benefits, such as the status that party politicians derive from occupying positions of authority in the state--are as important incentives for political action in the modern state as in any other. Indeed a good argument can be made that various "selective incentives" are required, in addition to the desired public goods (or feared public evils) that policies produce, to arouse sufficient interest in policies to secure their adoption.[61] This may be particularly true when it comes to leadership--to those persons who do most of the political "work" that makes a policy realizable. It is nevertheless true that the primary purpose of modern politics is to secure more favorable (or less unfavorable) policies, and that the modern vocabulary of politics, which is very much a vocabulary of interest in policies, of the equity or inequity of policies, and of the technical requirements of policies, is a fairly good indication of this.

Policy government is not necessarily a regime of group or class equality. Policies ordinarily are aimed at open, achieved categories within general publics, but not all categories will be acknowledged or given the same degree of attention by policymakers. Many categories of persons with common interests in public policy, especially those without organization and leaders, will be "forgotten." The central point of Olson's argument is that there are, in a modern plural polity, many "unorganized groups" that "have no lobbies and exert no pressure" and may even "have no tendency voluntarily to act to further their common interests."[62] Even among those that are organized, there are differences in their abilities to influence policies. But a further point about the modern state, as we have seen, is that there is a need for its policies to be justifiable with reference to the general public. This means that policies can be criticized on grounds of inequality, and that inequalities supported by public policies are not justifiable, even if they seem unavoidable. (It is the attempted justification of such

---

[61] Olson, p. 51.

[62] Ibid., p. 165.

policies that makes the racist regimes of Rhodesia and South Africa so morally outrageous to the modern world.) It also means that policies concerned with equality are likely to be deliberately developed: progressive taxation policies, regional equalization policies, welfare policies, and so on.

Where equality is critical to a regime of policy government--where it is noncontroversial and therefore nonpolitical--is within the achieved categories of persons who constitute the typical domains of policy. If one qualifies to belong to a category, one has the right to receive the benefits of a policy equally with all others who qualify, or the duty to bear the burdens of a policy equally. It is in the interstices of policy rules and procedures that many of the nonpolitical, and usually individual, issues of inequity and injustice arise. These tend to be nonpolitical issues because they deal with the application of policies to particular cases within some category. The injustices that rule applications give rise to are typically the problems not of politicians so much as judges, administrators, "ombudsmen," and the like. In a regime of policy government, political disputes are more often about the writing of policy rules and their general application than about the details of their application in particular cases. Indeed, policy government is a political regime that is distinguished by its remarkable success in removing issues of rule application from the political process--by its removing politics from administration (in this sense). It is precisely this separation that is not characteristic of a government regime of an underdeveloped country, as we shall see.

Public Administration

Modern policy government is bureaucratic government on an unprecedented scale: equitable policies seem to require bureaucratic administration. This relationship has been a source of great controversy among political theorists as well as politicians in the modern state. As policies have become more elaborate and ambitious, the bureaucratic apparatus of government has expanded.

A striking trait of the modern polity in recent generations and throughout modern times has been a vast expansion in the scope of policy. The pattern of policy has grown in both variety and magnitude, more functional areas being differentiated and the total output itself increasing.[63]

---

[63] Beer, Modern Political Development, p. 53.

The growth of policy also has meant a great expansion in the
size and scope of government: in the government share of the
gross domestic product, in the size of government budgets, in
the variety, scale, and complexity of public organizations, in
public employment as a proportion of total employment, and in
the variety of specially qualified officials and "experts" who
staff and operate the great public bureaus. Modern government
is preeminently a system of complex, diversified, and large-
scale administrative enterprises which coordinate great staffs
of officials in an effort to implement the collective decisions
established in public policies.

Policy government requires some system of instrumental
administration so that the policies framed at the higher levels
of government can be carried out at the lower levels. Collective
decisions and policies meant to apply equitably to categories
of persons require rules, regulations, and procedures that are
enforceable; otherwise government would become arbitrary, and
"policies" in effect would be set largely at the personal
discretion of government officials. Under such circumstances,
only some kind of highly indoctrinated officialdom--such as
Plato's guardians--could prevent the deterioration of administration into a system of personal and arbitrary rule. In an
organization staffed by ordinary mortals, a procedural and
impersonal type of administration characteristic of "bureaucracy" usually must be relied on to implement the collective
decisions that typify policy government.

Bureaucracy (as noted) is impersonal and procedural.
Procedures typically are incorporated into the administrative
process as sets of routines. In a famous study Robert Merton
has observed that bureaucratic structure can implant itself in
the personalities of officials, who may come to exhibit over-
conformity with procedures and routines. Merton is critical
of the bureaucratic personality who, in extreme cases, sacrifices
efficiency and flexibility at the individual level for the sake
of conformity with general rules.[64] Bureaucratic administration
undoubtedly exhibits these as well as other "pathological"
characteristics, which are recognized in ordinary language by
the pejorative definition of "bureaucracy" as "a system of
administration marked by officialism, red tape and proliferation" [Webster]. No system of administration is without its
costs, and in government, as elsewhere, costs are usually paid
or justified only in relation to the benefits or utilities they
promote. The important costs of bureaucracy that common language
recognizes are its impersonality, aloofness, and proceduralism.

---

[64]Robert K. Merton, Social Theory and Social Structure (Glencoe:
The Free Press, 1957), pp. 195-206.

The benefit that is generally noted by political and organizational theorists is the capacity of bureaucracy to administer large-scale societies with uniformity and equity. Individuals see the procedures and paperwork of bureaucracy, such as the numerous forms that have to be filled in properly and the delay and difficulty in getting an official answer to a question, and conclude that "bureaucrats" are inefficient and preoccupied with "red tape." From the broader perspective of public policy, it is precisely the routine procedures and paperwork--the treatment of individuals as cases within categories--which ensures against arbitrariness or interference in policy administration. Proceduralism and impersonality are essential.

> [A]ny system which deals with individual cases so as to take full account of the individual human situation will almost inevitably be slower and more complicated. By losing impersonality, it will also run the risk of encouraging nepotism and corruption.[65]

This, of course, is precisely the problem in government in underdeveloped countries.

Ideally and very often in reality, modern public bureaucracies are staffed by officials and experts who hold their posts exclusively by considerations of merit. At the highest administrative levels of the modern state, where much of the policymaking activity takes place, and in the specialized ministries required for the pursuit of technically demanding public purposes, the concentration of expertise is without historical precedent. At almost all levels of modern public administration, considerations of merit weigh heavily in staff recruitment and advancement; even postmen must pass examinations as a condition of public employment. In Western countries the past century has witnessed the virtually universal acceptance (if it was not accepted everywhere before) of J.S. Mill's argument that modern government is peculiarly dependent upon the employment of skilled and expert officials:

> The entire business of government is skilled employment; the qualifications for the discharge of it are of that special and professional kind which cannot be properly judged of except by persons who have themselves some share of those qualifications, or some practical experience of them.[66]

---

[65]R.S. Milne, "Decision-Making in Developing Countries," Journal of Comparative Administration, Vol. 4 (February 1972), p. 394.

[66]John Stuart Mill, Utilitarianism, On Liberty, and Considera-

If modern government is a serious and complex business, it cannot rely upon an avocational administration consisting, especially at its highest levels, mainly of the wellborn. For Mill it requires an altogether different aristocracy--an "aristocracy of talent," or what has come to be called a "meritocracy." What distinguishes policy government from all other types is not the fact of merit--merit has been a consideration of administration in English government, for instance, since pre-modern times[67]--but the principle that all other considerations, ideally, should be excluded.

Policies require experts, and experts acquire an abiding interest in policies--especially those dependent upon their expertise. The vested interests experts attach to the policies they help fashion and administer are not the same as the vested interests avocational administrators attach to the possession of administrative offices for their own sake. Experts desire to hold a monopoly of skill and expertise; avocational administrators desire to possess a right of incumbency, and in some cases a right of possession, an entitlement.

Public administration by experts and professionally qualified officials is not policy-neutral, as the dogmatists of the separation of politics and administration sometimes have asserted. Many public policies in the modern state are conceived, and most are elaborated and implemented, by the efforts of expert and experienced officials who staff the public bureaus. As Norton Long puts it:

> In many fields . . . the staff work on which well-conceived public policy must depend can scarcely be supplied elsewhere than in the great government departments. . . . The view of administration as sheerly instrumental, or even largely instrumental, must be rejected as empirically untenable and ethically unwarranted.[68]

---

tions on Representative Government (London: J.M. Dent, 1910), pp. 335-36.

[67]Wolfram Fischer and Peter Lundgreen, "The Recruitment and Training of Administrative and Technical Personnel" in Charles Tilly, ed., The Formation of National States in Western Europe (Princeton: Princeton University Press, 1975), pp. 456-561.

[68]"Public Policy and Administration: The Goals of Rationality and Responsibility," Public Administration Review, Vol. XIV (Winter 1954), pp. 23, 55.

Such a view rejects an older one associated not only with Woodrow
Wilson, but also with the earlier utilitarians, with James Mill
and Jeremy Bentham, who believed that the expert official
"simply decides on the most efficient way of realizing the will
of the legislature."[69] Since policies depend on their expertise,
and since experts have a vested interest in fostering such
policy dependence, they cannot be expected to be neutral about
the policies and programs they help to develop and administer.
No system of policy government could be expected to be free of
such partisanship, and it is doubtful that any policy-neutral
bureaucracy or bureaucrat has ever existed in the world of public
administration, particularly at the higher levels. Lindblom
has argued that public administrators not only are among the
most "proximate" of policy advocates, but that at the highest
levels of government, "administrators inevitably make policy."[70]
Policy--certainly the details of policy--must be a bureaucratic
passion if it is seriously expected to be implemented. And
policy advocacy does not violate the principle of the separation
of politics and administration: the politics that violate that
principle are the politics of party support or of loyalty to
particular politicians. It is this type of political partisanship that was eliminated by the civil service reforms of most
Western governments. (Perhaps this distinction can be seen more
clearly in academic communities, where on the one hand is found
the altogether desirable partisanship in support of contesting
viewpoints or theories, and on the other hand the unscholarly
practice, usually disguised, of political ideology advocacy.)

Consequently, it is not out of place to speak of the
"politics of bureaucracy" in modern government, by which is
meant a politics of policy or program advocacy involving arguments and debates among public officials with vested interests
in different policies and programs. Typically, such political
quarrels take place among different ministries or departments
over such matters as budget or recruitment policies or (what
often amounts to the same thing) areas of program expansion or
contraction. In parliamentary systems, the desire of senior
officials to have a strong and sympathetic minister to represent
departmental interests in the cabinet is not inconsistent with
the concept of a bureaucratic political process. Typical of the
analytic character of modern, policy government, political
contests in bureaucracies are fought with the paraphernalia of

---

[69]Alan Ryan, "Utilitarianism and Bureaucracy: The Views of
J.S. Mill" in Gilliam Sutherland, ed., Studies in the Growth
of Nineteenth-Century Government (London: Routledge & Kegan
Paul, 1972), p. 58.

[70]Lindblom, The Policy-Making Process, pp. 75-78.

policy: with reasoned arguments based upon submitted reports,
plans, statistics, and the like. Even when such contests turn
upon personalities, upon struggles among ambitious officials who
are determined "empire builders," the conflicts cannot be settled
definitively or final decisions justified without making reference
to policy arguments or considerations. Those personalities who
can make the most convincing and forceful policy arguments are
likely, under a regime of policy government, to be the most
effective bureaucratic politicians.

Non-Policy Government

The concepts and the vocabulary we use to analyze and
evaluate political conduct commit us to particular understandings:

The concepts we have settle for us the form of the experience
we have of the world. The world is for us what is presented
through those concepts. That is not to say that our concepts may not change; but when they do, that means that our
concept of the world has changed too.[71]

What can be said of concepts can also be said of words: the
world we experience is determined not only by our conceptions
of it, but also by the words we use to describe it. In this
and subsequent sections, I want to elaborate on the limits of
the modern vocabulary of policy government for understanding
political and administrative conduct in a typical non-Western,
plural society. I shall try to show how the vocabulary of
patronage is more suitable for such an understanding.

The vocabularies of culture and society, and most certainly of politics and government, are normative in two important
respects. They are normative in the sense that there must be
agreement and hence standards concerning the uses and meanings
of the words included in them; otherwise they could not have
entered the currency of language. All vocabularies--cultural,
social, political, legal, scientific, technical, and so on--are
normative in this sense. But the vocabularies of culture,
society, politics, and government are normative in the additional
sense of serving to convey impressions--sometimes correct, sometimes incorrect--of the contextual norms of the situation they
label or describe. Politicians, as we all know, are particularly
adept at exploiting this property of language by using words
quite deliberately to convey an impression that casts approval

---

[71]Peter Winch, The Idea of a Social Science (London: Routledge
& Kegan Paul, 1963), p. 23.

upon their own actions or policies and disapproval upon the conduct of their opponents. Since political and sociological vocabularies are normative in this second sense, academic analysts--particularly cross-cultural comparativists--are saddled with the challenge of using words and vocabularies in such ways that they do not suggest contextual norms that are not operative in a polity or society. The widespread use by academics of the vocabulary of policy government in the discussion and analysis of contemporary underdeveloped countries has not enabled them to avoid this difficulty.

The importance of the pluralistic social and cultural context in the study of such countries, and the restrictions such a context places on the use by political analysts of the vocabulary of policy government, can be illustrated by pursuing our analysis of the concept of "policy" one step further. "Policies" must be distinguished from "particular acts." More analytically, a policy

> consists not simply of a decision to give A ten pounds a week but to give everyone in such-and-such conditions ten pounds a week. Most laws are "policies" in this sense.[72]

Policies never particularize persons: they stipulate qualifications by which individuals can claim to belong to the policy domain. Qualifications may be almost anything so long as they can be achieved. Ascribed characteristics--such as race or sex-- ordinarily are not considered to be qualifications, although efforts have recently been made by the federal government in the United States to employ the concept of what Glazer calls "affirmative discrimination" with respect to minorities and women (and have caused serious political, legal, and moral controversy).[73] It is uncharacteristic for policies to particularize precisely because particularism entails discrimination or favoritism. In legal vocabularies particular acts have been assigned special labels to distinguish them from general acts, from "law" (and by implication, "policy"). Rousseau distinguishes

---

[72]Barry, p. 197.

[73]According to Glazer, affirmative action has come to mean "the setting of statistical requirements based on race, color, and national origin for employers and educational institutions. This new course threatens the abandonment of our concern for individual claims to consideration on the basis of justice and equity, now to be replaced with a concern for rights for public-ly determined and delimited racial and ethnic groups" (Nathan Glazer, Affirmative Discrimination: Ethnic Inequality and Public Policy [New York: Basic Books, 1975], p. 197).

"decrees" from "laws"[74]--a distinction that has wide application
to the acts of government in contemporary underdeveloped coun-
tries--and Barry notes that "laws which specify individuals to
be punished are distinguished as 'acts of attainder' (and prohibited under the US Constitution)."[75]

We have already analyzed how modern government operates
by means of public policymaking, by means of rules and procedures
which authorize and give direction to the conduct of officials.
Public policies ordinarily give expression to the substantive
aims of government and, often, the substantive interests of
politically organized groups in society; the domains of policy
are usually categorical groups of qualified individuals (or
similar agents, such as corporations) among the citizenry. I
have tried to show that it is difficult to operate a system of
policy government in a communally divided society because the
concepts of "policy" and "communal interest" are categorically
different. I have suggested that modern governments typically
respond to a communal group's interest in preserving its "way
of life" by guaranteeing special rights or immunities to the
community or by establishing a separate jurisdiction (for instance, a provincial or local government) for it. By virtue of
separate jurisdictions, it is possible for systems of policy
government to operate within communal populations without being
discriminatory: members of other communities who might otherwise qualify do not have to be considered because they belong
to other jurisdictions. But what about contexts in which
communities do not enjoy separate jurisdictions or special
constitutional protections? If policy is an inappropriate
concept in such a context, how should government actions be
conceived with respect to communal interests and concerns? What
is the appropriate vocabulary? I shall argue that the appropriate
vocabulary for analyzing a system of non-policy government is
the vocabulary of political patronage.

Non-policy government can be conceived to operate in
plural societies by means of patronage acts, by means of spoils
and preferments, that take account of the particular situations
of persons and communities. Though logically and linguistically
interdependent, the vocabularies of policy and patronage are

---

[74]"For will either is, or is not, general; it is the will
either of the body of the people, or only of a part of it. In
the first case, the will, when declared, . . . constitutes law:
in the second, it is merely a particular will, or act of magis-
tracy--at the most a decree" (The Social Contract, trans. G.D.H.
Cole [New York: E.P. Dutton, 1950], p. 24).

[75]Barry, p. 197.

quite distinctive and imply very different contextual norms. I
believe that it is possible to gain a better understanding of
the contrasting character of government in developed and underdeveloped countries by exploring some of these normative differences in detail. The discussion which follows rests on the
premise that "policy" and "patronage" are inversely related
concepts, which is consistent with the generally accepted view
that political development entails a decline in the proportion
of "patronage" to "policy" actions of government (a development
indicated normatively by the increasing identification of
patronage as an illegitimate form of government activity).
While agreeing with this general view, we should not be misled
into thinking that patronage is some kind of deformity on the
body politic: rather it is an alternative to policy government
that operates in accordance with quite different norms (whatever
we may think of them) and a different political logic. The
vocabulary of patronage can tell us something about these norms
and this logic.

Spoils and Preferments

Policy government is public government. Public policies
are formulated, deliberated, debated, adopted, announced, enforced. To be enforced they must be known, just as the law is
known (or at least is not concealed, and thus is assumed to be
known). Government policies directed at categorical groups or
the "public-at-large" must be "publicized" in order to be
complied with or in other ways responded to. Some policies
are not publicized because the government of the day does not
favor them, but approved policies which require the specific
cooperation of categories of persons (and many public policies
require such cooperation) by their very intent must be publicized.
Policy government frequently is government by public announcement
or advertisement, and the failure of particular policies often
is attributable to their lack of publicity.

Policies suggest choice and therefore inspire debates--
not necessarily in the press or in assemblies (where these exist
and enjoy some degree of independence)--but certainly within
the executive councils of modern government and often at the
higher levels of the civil and military services where policymaking is a preoccupation. Policy discussion and debate involves
deliberation, consideration, and what has been called "reasoned
argument." Public opinion is often opinion about policies,
proposed or extant. For opinions to be valid they usually
require reasons, which often reflect political viewpoints based
on moral principles, ideological convictions, professional concerns, economic interests, and so on. Policies need not respond
to such opinion, but when they are announced they usually must
be accompanied by reasoned arguments and justifications.

(Paradoxical as it may seem, not all public policies in the
modern state can be publicly announced. Modern governments
are often secretive with respect to those policies judged most
critical to the "national interest"--for instance, defense policy
or foreign policy. As Weber once observed:

> The tendency toward secrecy in certain administrative fields
> follows their material nature: everywhere that the power
> interests of the domination structure toward the outside
> are at stake, whether it is an economic competition of a
> private enterprise, or a foreign, potentially hostile
> polity, we find secrecy. If it is to be successful, the
> management of diplomacy can only be publicly controlled
> to a very limited extent. The military administration
> must insist on the concealment of its most important
> measures. . . .[76]

But secrecy, be it noted, has itself become an issue in modern
policy government, and must be publicly justified by reasoned
arguments.)

Government by spoils and preferments tends to be "private
government," both in the sense that government offices are treated
as private property and in the sense that spoils, unlike policies,
must be managed in a discreet and even a clandestine fashion.
Spoils are not officially announced so much as privately bestowed.
They cannot be advertised, and they cannot be publicly debated.
Spoils can be an issue for public debate, indeed for public
criticism, but only by judging them in terms of modern legal
and policy norms. This often is done by "modern" groups--
typically the intelligentsia--who usually hold government by
spoils to be wrong in principle.

Following Webster's definition of "debate" as "a discussion, especially of a public question in an assembly," it might
be more accurate to suggest that spoils provoke disputes rather
than debates. Spoils systems occasion disputes regarding access
to the spoils and the privileges surrounding such access. The
allocation of spoils is likely to provoke quarrels if they are
divided in full public view; for this reason it cannot be announced or declared. Spoils are not dividends, and unlike
policies, the division of spoils is not made with an eye upon
a future, more desirable state. Typically, the divider of
spoils is a reconciler rather than a steersman. Spoils are
present rewards for past services or favors that were provided

---

[76] H. Gerth and C. Wright Mills, eds., From Max Weber: Essays
in Sociology (New York: Oxford University Press, 1958), p. 223.
[Emphasis in original.]

in anticipation of gaining a share of the spoils. For this
reason participants in spoils systems have tended to be regarded
as "mercenaries" (which they often were in the earliest meaning
of spoils as the "spoils of war"). Disputes and disputants
arise with respect to the division of spoils: who shall be
rewarded and to what extent?

The politics of spoils is a type of distributive politics,
and the division of spoils raises distributive issues for individuals and groups inside a spoils system, or wishing to be inside
it. One easily recognized distributive issue raised by a spoils
system is that of political expediency: what is the most expedient division of the spoils that can meet the interests of participants so as to maintain their conditional support? But
spoils systems, particularly since they deal with substantive
wants, also raise the issue of distributive justice: can the
politically expedient division of the spoils--perhaps reflecting
the power of the participants--be justified against the informal
rights of participants to secure rewards commensurate with their
contribution to the victory? Spoils systems usually are seen as
pure politics of expedience (as though such a politics could
exist), but this leaves out of consideration the question of
distributive justice that tends to arise in the division of the
spoils.

The fact that spoils systems have been largely eliminated
through reforms in the Western democracies, and now are almost always evaluated from the perspective of modern, policy government,
has undoubtedly contributed greatly to the view of spoils systems
as necessarily unjust. To the modern political mind, the preferments and favors of a spoils system inevitably imply privilege and
injustice. Indeed, spoils always are bestowed with some concept
of preferment or partiality in mind: "To the victor belong the
spoils!" The logic of distribution in a spoils system is based
upon discrimination among supporters and contributors according to
the significance of the role each played in achieving victory. A
supporter makes a claim upon the spoils by calling attention to
past efforts; ideally, one's share of the spoils should be commensurate with one's efforts. Insofar as there is a conception of
justice within a spoils system, it is a conception of justice as
desert. Spoils are not divided or distributed arbitrarily: differences in the division and allocation of spoils have to be justified in terms of prior contributions. From the viewpoint of
policy government, spoils systems are unjust for failing to take
account of other merits than prior contributions (such as qualifications for holding office) or prior rights (such as citizenship).
But within a culture in which there is an understanding that
government favoritism is to be expected, and that it is unfair not
to extend preferment to individuals or groups who have aided (or
are aiding) the persons or party in power, the absence of favoritism is not only an injustice but perhaps even a betrayal.

By the same token, it is not an injustice to refuse to allocate spoils and patronage to persons and communities who failed to lend prior support. In a spoils system, as in gambling, winners take all, and the fairness of this division cannot be questioned by the losers. Injustice arises only when those who aided the winners are denied their fair share (in practice this is usually their perception of a fair share) of the spoils. Political support without preferment (or, more accurately, without commensurate preferment) is unjust. Thus in the Kenya National Assembly many of the post-independence disputes concerning "tribalism" in the allocation of government jobs arose from the allegation that one "tribe" within the ruling coalition--the Kikuyu--was receiving a disproportionate share of the spoils of the national independence victory.[77] In character with the ethics of a spoils system, some Kikuyu sought to justify such preferment by claiming--not entirely without reason--that Kenyan independence was primarily, perhaps exclusively, a Kikuyu achievement.

In some underdeveloped countries, unusual tactics have been employed in attempts to gain entitlement to spoils. In African legislatures it is not uncommon for newly elected members of "opposition" parties to "cross the floor" and sit with the winners in the (faint) hope of making a claim upon the spoils of electoral victory. For example, at the first meeting of the Somalia National Assembly following the elections of March 1969--an election contested by 62 parties, most of them one-man lineage parties--all but one of the elected opposition members crossed the floor to join the governing party.[78] For a legitimate claim upon the division of the spoils to be made, or a protest against the injustice of their distribution, some kind of prior contribution is required. If we are amused by the behavior of the opposition members of the Somalian Assembly, it is from the recognition that when political support is extended only at the eleventh hour (or the thirteenth), it has little or no moral force. Somewhere in the theory of the "political bandwagon" is the principle that those who contribute their efforts earliest, when the outcome is most in doubt, are entitled to claim the greatest preferments if and when victory has been won; as time passes and the prospects for victory grow increasingly bright, the value of "new" support (and hence the right to claim a share of the spoils) is correspondingly diminished.

---

[77]Cherry Gertzel, Maure Goldschmidt, and Donald Rothchild, eds., Government and Politics in Kenya (Nairobi: East African Publishing House, 1969), pp. 41-51.

[78]I.M. Lewis, "The Politics of the 1969 Somali Coup," Journal of Modern African Studies, Vol. 10 (October 1972), p. 397.

Personal Administration

Policy government entails impersonal, bureaucratic administration. Along with the important role played by public officials in the "development" of policies, their roles of "implementing" and "enforcing" policies are essential to the viability of any system of policy government. On the other hand, patronage government is unworkable--indeed inconceivable--with a system of public administration. The "legalism" of bureaucratic administration--the preoccupation of bureaucrats with rules, procedures, and routines--is sharply at odds with the personalism, discrimination, and favoritism of a patronage system. Government officials would have to be free to disregard rules to make a patronage system work, and an administration of officials who consistently disregarded rules and procedures would not be a bureaucratic administration.

Policies, we have seen, can be conceived as authoritative instructions to public officials whose duty it is to implement or enforce them. Policy government can permit the exercise of discretionary authority by officials only insofar as it is required for the implementation or enforcement of policies. In practice, the administration of public policies, like the interpretation of legal rules, requires what can be called rule or procedural discretion (acknowledged in the legal concept of "equity"), which permits adjustments in the application of rules or policies that would result in the unequal treatment of equals--but it cannot countenance discretion to disregard the rules. The connection between legal "equity" and discretion, as Carl Friedrich notes, can be traced to Aristotle's dictum that justice requires discretion for judges but only within a framework of rules:

> The same holds within organizations between superiors and inferiors who are given discretion, and are expected to "explain" by sufficient reasoning why they decided as they did.[79]

As Hart observes, discretion may be necessary but it should always be "reasonable": every discretionary action must be justifiable in relation to the law or to a policy.[80] Even undertaken for the most altruistic of reasons or for a personal conception of the public good, the exercise of authority by an official in knowing violation of administrative regulations is

---

[79]*Tradition and Authority* (London: Pall Mall Press, 1972), pp. 68-69.

[80]Hart, pp. 128-29.

indefensible. Just as legal norms governing the conduct of
judges have been built up to protect the law, bureaucratic norms
are intended to protect policy from any interference by those
officials entrusted with its implementation and enforcement.

Discretionary conduct in non-bureaucratic administration
is quite different. It is not the discretionary acts of responsible, rule-minded officials; it is not action justified in
relation to policy. It is more like the personal discretion of
possession or entitlement providing officials with something
akin to proprietary rights in respect of their authority and
actions. If we want a model, Weber's concept of "patrimonial
administration," with its aura of personalism, is suggestive.
Weber uses a negation of this concept to convey his sense of
the nature of bureaucracy:

> It [bureaucracy] does not constitute a realm of _free,_
> arbitrary action, of mercy, and of _personally_ motivated
> favour and valuation, as we shall find to be the case
> among pre-bureaucratic forms.[81]

Under a regime of personal administration, the official is freed
from the constraints and protections of administrative procedures
and placed in a position where other influences, other interests,
and other obligations can be brought to bear on his conduct--in
a position where his extra-official interests, sympathies, and
responsibilities can be appealed to.

But personal administration is not wholly arbitrary
administration (as Weber sometimes implies). The personal
discretion that permits the official to act without the restraint
of bureaucratic rules is not a license to act egotistically.
Freedom of the official from bureaucratic constraints and duties
does not mean that he is free from other constraints and duties.
Indeed, the opposite is more likely. Freedom from bureaucratic
controls is also freedom from bureaucratic protections--specifi-
cally the protections of the rules and regulations which provide
officials with valid reasons for denying extra-bureaucratic
claims on their authority. And there are likely to be extra-
bureaucratic claims, particularly if the official possesses
authority that can facilitate the realization of the substantive
wants or needs of individuals or groups in the society. Thus,
in the vocabulary of this study, freedom from the official constitution implies nothing in the way of freedom from the social
constitution of the underlying plural society.

The rules and logic of personal administration can also
be viewed, and perhaps brought into sharper focus, from the

---

[81]Gerth and Mills, eds., p. 220. [Emphasis in original.]

standpoint of conflict-of-interest theory. This theory holds
that public office imposes upon an incumbent official a prior duty
or responsibility to the general public or its representative.
The exercise of discretionary authority--and for many officials,
especially senior policy-advising officials, much of their authority is discretionary--must not be inconsistent with official
duties or that aspect of the "public interest" that the office
exists to serve. The official must never place his own personal/
private interests, or those of his family, friends, or non-of-
ficial associates, or any other third-party interest before his
public duty, should they come into conflict. Conflict-of-interest
theory generally does not allow even the potential for such a
conflict by insisting that public officials divest themselves
of private business interests, and the spirit of the conflict-
of-interest prohibition dictates that public officials sufficient-
ly separate themselves from third-party interests to avoid even
the suspicion of a conflict of interest. Beyond their salaries
and other official emoluments, public officials are prohibited
from gaining materially from their positions.

This theory fits badly with patronage government and its
system of personal administration because it assumes that the
impersonal norms of "officiality" and the "separation" of public
and private are operative. Insofar as the term "official" has
meaning in the context of personal administration, it is mainly
as a label borne by a class of persons; it cannot be used to
discriminate between the different kinds of actions they engage
in. Rather than being agents of government in their official
capacities, officials are the government; whatever such officials
do or say in such a system is official. Most systems of authoritarian government are roughly of this character. A conception
of incumbency as a kind of "ownership" robs the public/private
distinction of meaning. It contrasts sharply with the assumption of conflict-of-interest theory that government offices are
"public property."

In a plural society with a system of personal administration, an official's primary public duty may be to members of his
own community or to the para-public community interest. Obvious-
ly the question of public duty hinges on the conception of the
"public," and in a pluralistic society that public is at least
as likely to be some kind of subnational community as the pan-
societal, general public. In such a context, conflict-of-interest theory is confused and quite misleading: the conflict is
no longer one of personal- or private-regarding action versus
public-oriented action, of private interest versus public duty.
Rather it is a conflict of competing public duties, of contrasting social norms.

Modern theories of government, I have been suggesting,
are intent upon analyzing and evaluating official conduct from

the teleocratic perspective of the public interest and in relation to the policies and procedures which, in practice, issue from such a perspective. While procedural discretion is allowed, officials (if called upon to do so) are required to give reasons for their actions that are consistent with official policy. Regulations and reasonableness constitute, as it were, the two cords binding the official to the state: he may sever them only at the risk of imperiling his official position. The official's duty is a public duty in the sense that the regulations and reasons governing his conduct issue from or must be justified to some higher, ultimately "sovereign" authority.

The essential inadequacy of this perspective for the analysis and evaluation of administrative conduct in communally divided polities is its inability to discern, with sufficient precision, the nature of the conflicts of duty confronting government officials in such polities. To view all conduct in violation of official policy and administrative procedure as illegitimate is to assume the validity of using the general public interest as the exclusive standard for making such judgments, and to overlook the degree of pluralism in public morals. The alternative perspective offered in this study enables us to recognize that what may be illegitimate from the viewpoint of the nation-state or with reference to the general public may be quite legitimate from the viewpoint of a community or with reference to some para-public within a society. More than this, it enables us to see that the action may be illegitimate or legitimate from both viewpoints. Indeed our analytical ability to make normative distinctions is quadrupled, for what was a right/wrong distinction from the first perspective becomes, from the alternative perspective of the communal polity, the more complex equation: right/wrong, wrong/right, right/right, and wrong/wrong. The analysis of patronage and corruption which follows will elaborate on these distinctions in the context of the theory of government in underdeveloped societies.

Chapter IV

PATRONAGE AND CORRUPTION

I shall not take issue with what appears to be overwhelming evidence of political patronage and "corruption" in
the governments of underdeveloped countries, but I do want to
comment on the interpretation of such practices. The quotation
marks around the word "corruption" call attention to the fact
that our conception of what constitutes corrupt practices is
almost wholly dependent upon our point of view and the standards
we use to evaluate conduct. Administrative and political conduct
that is condemned as corrupt in one society at one time may not
be corrupt in another society or at another time. Standards
change, and often the so-called incidence of corruption is
not so much a function of changing behavior as of revised
standards. I suspect that much of the evidence of a recent
increase in corrupt practices in Western countries may very
well be the consequence of higher standards and a lowering of
public tolerance of certain forms of conduct. It is also possible that practices that are judged corrupt from one standpoint
or in relation to a particular reference group may not be considered corrupt if the standpoint or reference group is changed.
In a sense, "corruption" is created by our conceptions of it.

The analysis and evaluation of patronage and corruption
in plural societies only from the standpoint of public government
or by reference to the general public risks being both one-sided
and misleading. Such a perspective will mislead if it discounts
the existence and validity of other standpoints and reference
groups. If these are taken into account, we may decrease our
moral certainty, but our analytical ability to draw distinctions
will be increased. We will begin to apprehend something of the
uncertainty and ambiguity surrounding the choice of political
standpoints and reference groups that besets political actors
in underdeveloped countries. One is reminded of Barry's observation that

> just as problems of a conflict of loyalties give rise to
> some of the most intractable problems of personal morals,
> so problems of which reference group to take into account
> provide many of the most intractable political problems[82]

--and (I would add) analytical problems as well.

---

[82]Barry, p. 13.

In comparative analysis involving underdeveloped countries, the scholar must refrain from deriving his analyses and
evaluations solely from the standpoint of a modern nation-state.
By analyzing what appear to be "corrupt" practices only from the
standpoint of the moral and legal principles of a national political community, the scholar is in danger of establishing "corruption" by his concepts alone; the moral principles of other
communities may justify such conduct by the individuals involved.
By assuming the existence of a plurality of reference groups,
which is characteristic of a non-Western plural society, and
the possibility of moral dilemmas arising because of the con-
flicting standards of these groups, a political theorist stands
a better chance of avoiding this danger, and might very well
sharpen our definitions and conceptions of patronage and corruption.

Patronage

Defined generally as "a right of nomination" [Oxford],
and more specifically as the right "to make appointments to
government jobs on a basis other than merit alone" [Webster],
patronage entails a conception of administrative staffing
sharply at odds with the prevailing conception in the modern
nation-state. The modern conception is best revealed institu-
tionally in the establishment of official agencies--typically
"public service commissions"--whose agents are vested with the
authority to regulate the administrative recruitment process.
In a patronage system the "right of nomination" belongs not to
an impartial, procedure-minded body but to individuals who
usually hold elective or appointive office themselves, and are
in a position to exercise personal discretion in the appointment
of subordinates. Their personal and political judgment, rather
than the judgment of an agency impartially applying objective
and impersonal criteria, determines who shall be appointed.

Patronage systems do not necessarily ignore merit as a
criterion of administrative appointment, but the logic of
patronage is fundamentally at odds with the logic of a "meritocracy." The governing logic of a meritocracy dictates the
impartial application of impersonal and objective criteria in
recruitment decisions, the criteria themselves being determined
with a view toward promoting some aspect of the public interest--
typically efficient and publicly accountable administration.
As with the law, these criteria must be determined beforehand,
must be publicly announced, and must be applied impartially.
Generally speaking, to invent criteria afterwards to justify
an appointment, or to use private or secret criteria, would
be to violate the rule of merit. One important purpose of a
merit system is to remove such arbitrariness from the recruitment process.

The logic of a patronage system provides the nominator with the latitude to apply his own criteria, taking account of his particular situation. The privileges and the powers of nomination are not set apart or placed under official restrictions. The nominator's patronage rights and powers are not distinguished and separated from his other rights and powers. Rather, such rights and powers are an integral element of political authority--perhaps the key element in a government of spoils and preferments. Typically the criteria that dominate patronage systems are political favor and personal trust. (The vocabulary of patronage is characterized by terms of a political and personal nature.)

The logic of a patronage system allows personal discretion to the nominator, but not the license to appoint whomever he pleases. Patronage, after all, is a method of politics, and a patronage system--like any political system--can only operate by taking account of obligations and interests, by making normative appeals and extending positive satisfactions. A patron is an individual or representative of some group in a position to confer or withhold patronage according to his or their lights. But the point of employing patronage is to husband or enhance the patron's power, position, or prestige, as well as to promote his concerns. To dispense the favors and benefits of patronage arbitrarily or randomly would remove the power and prestige patronage elicits, since no individual or group clients henceforth could extend services and esteem to the patron in the confident expectation of being favored in return. Patronage is a conditional game of politics that is played according to distinctive rules.

Patronage games require that patrons possess a considerable degree of personal discretion. But such discretion is always bounded by norms, by conventions and understandings of some kind, as when electoral victory places a party leader in a position to bestow patronage, but prearranged understandings with lieutenants and supporters restrict his freedom to nominate. In dispensing presidential patronage, a newly elected U.S. president is often restricted by many understandings and promises arranged beforehand. If he fails to keep his promises, those who were supporters may very well turn into opponents (or at least nonsupporters), thereby reducing or threatening to reduce his position of electoral power in the future. When electoral coalitions are built by promises of spoils and preferments in the event of victory, the failure to keep such promises and distribute the spoils of victory in accordance with the ethics of desert will at the very least cast doubt and suspicion on the conduct and trustworthiness of the winner. No rational politician in a patronage game would wish to invite such doubt and suspicion by willfully breaking or ignoring the rules of the game. A political or administrative patron's discretion to dispense favors (or withhold them) must be conceived to be limited by the rules and understandings of whatever the particular patronage game happens to be.

Unlike merit systems, patronage regimes can take account of the personal considerations and communal concerns that loom so large in a plural society. It is appropriate for government officials who have patronage privileges to acknowledge their personal and communal obligations by nominating the favored sons and daughters of families and friends within their reference community to government posts. In this way the logic of a patronage system is inherently consistent with the norms of a communal polity; the logic of a merit system can be so only accidentally. It is not inconceivable (though it would be completely unintended) that appointment exclusively by merit could install the same communal clients in the same posts as would a patronage system, but the further purpose of patronizing additional members of the community--for instance, a client's kinsmen--would not be served. The merit appointee could place himself in a patronage position only by turning his back on the merit considerations that resulted in his own appointment.

A patronage system is not only (and perhaps not even primarily) a method of selecting individuals for government posts: it is not merely a system of recruitment. It is also an ongoing method of attending to the interests or prerogatives of communities and the influence or privileges of communal notables. Under such a system, officeholding is not only the result of patronage, but also the basis of future acts of patronage by the nominee in relation to his own community or that of his patron--likely the same one. By similar reasoning, but in relation to a very different reference group and with respect to the administration of policies rather than the assignment of spoils and preferments, the merit appointee is expected to impartially apply regulations that are designed to serve the interests of the general public or some open, categorical group within it. A patronage nominee who refused to honor his personal or communal obligations would, under a regime of patronage, be acting as irresponsibly as a merit appointee who violated his obligation to carry out faithfully and to the best of his abilities his duties to serve the general public.

A patronage nominee is no less accountable after his appointment than a merit appointee. He is, however, accountable to a very different kind of authority: the personal authority of his patron, upon whom he is henceforth dependent. This is the usual understanding of patronage accountability which is exemplified, for instance, in the "dependency relationships" of patrimonial-style administration[83] or in the more general practice by which an act or gift of patronage is understood to secure for the nominator the loyalty and dependence of his nominee. A

---

[83]Weber, III, pp. 1010-15.

system of patronage government is a complex network of personal ties and obligations between patrons and their clients, and there is no question that functioning, legitimate systems of government of this type can be and often have been built.

The political advantages of patronage are well known, and are still exploited in some political spheres of the modern nation-state--for instance, by elected leaders at all levels in their selection of aides and assistants, including national leaders, such as U.S. presidents, who exercise broad patronage powers in making senior administrative appointments and in nominating candidates for high posts in the judiciary and other appointive bodies. Certainly the vocabulary of patronage still has many uses in the analysis of modern government, but today we are apt to forget that not very long ago it was common for Western governmental systems to be run exclusively on a patronage basis. Sir Robert Walpole enjoys his place in English history not least for having governed England by his astute exercise of the Prime Minister's powers and privileges of patronage[84] (much to the dismay of Viscount Bolingbroke and the Tory opposition, who criticized the personal abuses and excesses of Walpole's patronage empire as a "Robinocracy" of ministerial and adminis-trative jobbery, bribery, and corruption: "a vast number of new dependents on the Crown").[85] In eighteenth-century England, patronage governance came to be associated not only with the traditional electoral privileges of landed magnates to influence the House of Commons by their right to nominate MP's, but also with a new, wealthy mercantile class who both provided the government with an unprecedented tax base for operating an elaborate system of administrative patronage and used its wealth to secure advantages from the government. If aristocratic patrons influenced the House of Commons through a gentlemen's understanding that required the resignation of a parliamentary client "if he parted company with his patron in his voting in Parliament,"[86] mercantile interests could use their private wealth to purchase influence both in the Commons and the adminis-tration. The effect of such a patronage system was to "privatize" government, making it an arena where the particular interests of prestigious and wealthy patrons could be served. If the government--acting in a manner typical of mercantilism--assisted

---

[84] J.H. Plumb, The Growth of Political Stability in England: 1675-1725 (Harmondsworth: Penguin Books, 1969), pp. 177-86.

[85] Viscount Bolingbroke, Political Writings, edited by Isaac Kramnick (New York: Appleton-Century-Crofts, 1970), pp. 21-33.

[86] Samuel Beer, British Politics in the Collectivist Age (New York: Alfred A. Knopf, 1965), p. 23.

the process by dealing widely in licenses, permits, and similar particularistic authorizations, Parliament assisted it by dealing mainly in private members bills. Numerous private bills that secured the particular interests of private patrons were passed by Parliament, and Beer comments that "the eighteenth century saw nothing striking, much less scandalous" in "all of this."[87]

The widespread practice of political and governmental patronage in underdeveloped countries suggests that the non-Western standpoint for evaluating political conduct may not be very different from this eighteenth-century English view. It is difficult to believe that policy government is anything approaching the norm in most of these countries, as widespread complaints of corruption and the failure of plans and policies attest. These complaints are, of course, the complaints of modernizers and state teleocrats--of intellectuals, of socialists, of planners and other social engineers--and are not too different from the kinds of complaints that began to be made against patronage regimes in Europe during the eighteenth and nineteenth centuries: a telling sign that modernization is, among other things, a normative contest of contrasting standards and viewpoints. In this respect, the numerous reports of government inquiries into political and administrative corruption in contemporary Asian and African countries is ample testimony of the normative dissonance of such countries with respect to the conception and legitimation of standards of public conduct. To the extent that widespread "public" complaints about patronage and corruption in such countries are matched by "private" acceptance and even approval--and I believe that this is what is generally occurring--then it seems likely that the ideal of patronage governance is still a normative force to be reckoned with.

Corruption

In a patronage system, political accountability entails not only the client's obligations to his patron but also his further obligation to assign the preferments and spoils within his power to dispose in line with his communal obligations, and to continue such activity on a more or less indefinite basis. Here we are approaching the wider conception of "patronage" characteristic of the technical use of this term in academic writing. A recent survey of such uses concludes with a definition of patronage as

---

[87]Ibid., p. 28.

the right vested in a person, official or political party
to appoint persons to offices and positions, to award
contracts, and to dispose of emoluments and other favours.[88]

This definition moves us into an area where the conceptions of
patronage and corruption may appear to overlap or even to merge,
but they are conceptually distinct.

The distinction between them is a distinction of authority, of officiality-legality, of morality, of right. Patronage
is "rightful" conduct; corruption is not. The exercise of
authority in a way that violates rules or regulations is misconduct which can be designated as "corrupt" conduct if it is
knowingly engaged in by an official for his own advantage or
for that of a third party favored by him. It is possible to
conceive of official conduct as discretionary--even arbitrary--
but not corrupt, so long as no rules or norms are transgressed.
Irregular conduct is not necessarily misconduct or corrupt
conduct. Before the conduct of an official can be classified as
misconduct, some known prohibition has to be violated. If such
conduct is willful violation of the rules for the sake of
private-personal advantage, or in order to unfairly or illegally
benefit some third party, then it can be regarded as an act of
"corruption" in the legal sense. However, if the rules proscrib-
ing such conduct are mere artifices--only nominally known and
not socially sanctioned--then it will be difficult to designate
the conduct as "corrupt." Genuine corruption entails the violation of some social standard. The definition of "corruption"
in the Dictionary of the Social Sciences takes account of this
consideration:

> Corruption in public life is the use of public power for
> private profit, preferment, or prestige, or for the benefit
> of a group or class, in a way that constitutes a breach of
> law or of standards of high moral conduct.[89]

Official rectitude or corruption can be conceived only
in relation to some reference group and the standards of public
propriety that are upheld within it. In the legal and political
theory of the modern state, the national citizenry is the valid
reference group, and the upward bureaucratic-executive-sovereign
chain of accountability is the system of authorized rules and
procedures against which official conduct is to be judged. A
self-serving or special interest-favoring action by an official
in violation of his rules of office or (amounting to the same

---

[88]Hugh Bone, "Patronage" in Gould and Kolb, eds., p. 486.

[89]Charles Aikin, "Corruption" in Gould and Kolb, eds., p. 142.

thing) his public duty is a typical instance of corruption in
the view of modern legal and political theory. Just as the
principle of an official's duty to the general public has assumed
validity in Western countries during the past century or two, so
also has the subordinate conception of a breach of public trust
and corruption assumed its present meaning.

Employed without suitable qualification, such a modern
conceptual perspective may mislead in the analysis and interpretation of corruption in government in underdeveloped societies.
This is recognized by Huntington:

> Behavior which was acceptable and legitimate according to
> traditional norms becomes unacceptable and corrupt when
> viewed through modern eyes. Corruption in a modernizing
> society is thus in part not so much the result of the devi-
> ance from accepted norms as it is the deviance of norms
> from the established patterns of behavior. New standards
> and criteria of what is right and wrong lead to a condemna-
> tion of at least some traditional behavior patterns as
> corrupt.[90]

But such a conception remains a lawyer's definition of corruption
rather than a social theorist's, so long as the new public
standards of official propriety are not socially valid. More-
over, if communal-type groups constitute for most people a
socially valid reference group, and if communal-type obligations
define the highest duty of government officials, then conduct
that is "corrupt" by modern legal definition might be "correct"
by traditional social convention. Again we encounter the central
moral dilemma of modernizing societies in which different standards of conduct come into conflict.

A conception of subnational reference groups and pluralistic rules of obligation will enable us to recognize that conduct
which is "corrupt" in relation to official rules and regulations
(hereafter "official corruption") may be not only acceptable but
obligatory from the standpoint of particular communities in
society. The same conception will enable us to see how legally
or procedurally correct conduct by officials may appear not only
as "arrogance" but as a rejection of communal rights when judged
from the communal point of view. The willful refusal of an official to honor his community's rules of mutual aid, even for
reasons of official rules and regulations, can be seen as a
rejection of his social obligations, provided he exercises some
discretion in the matter. (It might be noted in passing that
Gunnar Myrdal would, wherever possible, withhold such discretion

---

[90]Huntington, p. 60.

is resolved. To use the word "corruption" in such a context is to mistake moral awareness for immoral selfishness. It also is misleading to speak of "proto-corruption," defined as "pre-nineteenth-century practices which only became 'corrupt' in the nineteenth century."[93] Such a definition imposes an artificial standard, as Scott himself seems to acknowledge by the use of the prefix "proto" and the inverted commas around the word "corrupt." Both of these conceptions are misleading--the first by mistaking a moral conflict for a moral/interest conflict, and the second by applying the standards of one historical period to the circumstances of another. If these distinctions and criticisms are valid, it means that at least some of the corruption thought to be present in governments in underdeveloped countries is not there at all but is the result of errors in analysis, and also that such "corruption" is the consequence, at least some of the time, not of an official's venality but of his communal virtue. It also means that the problem of corruption is even more of a political and moral dilemma than it was thought to be.

There is one type of misconduct in governments in under-developed countries that is regarded as corruption in terms of both the official rules of the new state and the communal obliga-tions of the old society. This has been called "market corrup-tion" and is defined as "the [unlawful] selling of government goods and services to the highest bidder, whether he has 'connec-tions' or not."[94] A typical example is an extra "fee" that must be paid to an official before he will agree to issue a license or permit. The fee may be levied in addition to regular fees and after all regulations and other qualifications have been met by the applicant, or it may be a substitute fee to enable the applicant to avoid the regulations. Agencies in governments of underdeveloped countries which issue drivers' licenses, trading or business permits, building permits--even research clearances, as some scholars can attest--are typical arenas where market corruption can occur, the extra fee (often a pre-specified amount) constituting a bribe to the official(s) issuing them. Typical of market corruption is the payment of bribes to compen-sate for failing to qualify for permits, to jump queue, or to avoid or reduce taxes, fines, or other penalties or prohibitions. When such "market" forces penetrate government--the realm of the "collective"--the policy-procedural relationship between a public official and a citizen (involving an official's duty and a citizen's rights and obligations) is transformed into an unof-ficial and illegal market relationship between a seller and a

---

[93]Ibid., pp. 37-55.

[94]Ibid., p. 12.

buyer of a public permit or of protection from a public prohibition.

The sale of public authority, whether to the highest bidder or to those persons able to pay the going price, may be at odds not only with official regulations and policies but with traditional social obligations. Viscount Bolingbroke, the intellectual leader of the early eighteenth-century Tory opposition, was critical of Walpole's administration not because it violated modern public standards of equity and efficiency (which were not yet established) but because it violated the traditional standards of an aristocratic society by its "jobbing, pensioning, and buying of commoners."[95] An analogical type of corruption takes place in a contemporary non-Western plural society when officials insist upon the payment of market bribes by members of their own communities in violation of their communal duties. This type of practice points up what is essential to "market corruption": that it is a type of self-regarding or third-party favoring conduct that violates the social, legal, or moral rules of all reference groups. It also points up, correctly in my view, that corruption is particularly characteristic of societies undergoing a process of modernization, when different social norms and standards come into conflict with one another creating uncertainty in their wake.

Political development theorists have been ambivalent about "market corruption" because of a recognition that it may promote some aspects of economic modernization. Huntington has noted that

the corruption produced by the expansion of governmental regulation may stimulate economic development . . . [by] . . . surmounting traditional laws or bureaucratic regulations which hamper economic expansion.[96]

By cutting through red tape or overriding established customs, market corruption is seen to further economic modernization in those cases where the unrestrained agent is a modernizer intent on promoting modern values. In a carefully qualified argument, Nye has hypothesized that "top level corruption" by political elites may increase capital formation (and therefore investment and economic growth) if the capital is locally invested and not transferred abroad.[97] Both of these hypotheses posit a "trade-

---

[95]Bolingbroke, p. xv.

[96]Huntington, p. 68.

[97]J.S. Nye, "Corruption and Political Development: A Cost-

off" between unwelcome government regulations or traditional conventions and welcome economic developments, favoring economic gains even at the expense of official or social corruption.

To the extent that political development theorists are essentially concerned with the development of the new state as a universitas, as a system of public government (based on policymaking and public administration), it is necessary for them to show how market corruption can promote the development of public government. The logic and practice of government by public policymaking certainly cannot allow officials personal discretion to enforce policies as they see fit without requiring justification for such discretion. Nor can the scholar dismiss the premise of public government--if he is concerned about its development--whenever it appears to obstruct the attainment of other values, except by showing that the corruption or violation of present regulations is likely to result in the establishment of better regulations. Corruption may be one way of dealing with inappropriate or unwelcome regulations, perhaps prompting their reform, but a genuine concern about the development of viable and effective public institutions requires that the linkages between corruption and political development be shown. Bureaucracy may obstruct economic modernization by the regula-tions it places upon some kinds of economic activity, and other public institutions--for instance, the courts--may have similar effects, but within the premise of public government such prob-lems can ultimately be dealt with only by improved regulations (or administration) or better laws (or courts).

In general, the corruption-as-modernization thesis assumes a connection between economic modernization and the development of public government over the long run but without theorizing in specific terms about the linkages. Two political development theorists with an interest in corruption have at-tempted to provide such theories: Samuel Huntington and James Scott. Huntington has tried to show that corruption will con-tribute to net, long-term "political institutionalization" by weakening public bureaucracy while at the same time strengthen-ing political parties, which will nurture the kinds of collective interests that eventually will give rise to demands for policy government.[98] It is easy to see that corruption must weaken bureaucratic administration, since the two concepts are inversely related logically and linguistically, but the link between ad-ministrative corruption and the strengthening of political

---

Benefit Analysis," American Political Science Review, Vol. LXI (June 1967), p. 425.

[98]Huntington, pp. 69-71.

parties is more difficult to perceive. Two lines of argument are presented in support of the proposition that "some forms of corruption can contribute to political development by helping to strengthen political parties." In the first, "patronage" ("a mild form of corruption") has been used to build political parties, while in the second, corruption ("a product of moderniza- tion and . . . political participation") "requires the organiza- tion and structuring of that [political] participation."

Let us try to analyze these two lines of argument. Citing Harrington's assertion that "the corruption of one govern- ment . . . is the generation of another," Huntington advances the parallel argument that "the corruption [c] of one governmental organ [bureaucracy, hereafter X] contributes to the institution- alization [i] of another [political party, hereafter Y]." Or,

(1) cX contributes to iY,

in which case corruption is seen to vary directly with institu- tionalization, contrary to our usual understanding. Huntington has in mind the corruption of government bureaucracies by political leaders in order to secure funds to build their parties, citing the examples of Turkey, Mexico, Korea, Israel, India, West Africa, and "Communist parties." He then argues that effectively institutionalized political parties contribute to reduce overall corruption, or

(2) iY contributes to -cX,

since in general "corruption varies inversely with political organization." This proposition is consistent with our common understanding that corruption--as a mode of conduct (i.e., mis- conduct)--is antithetical to prescribed organizational roles and institutional rules, and that the introduction of organiza- tion usually has the effect of depersonalizing conduct and collectivizing interests. (In an organized political system comprising parties and interest groups, plural and collective nouns are essential to the language of political discourse.)

Taken at face value, proposition (2) contradicts propo- sition (1), which Huntington himself recognizes by adding the rider "in the long run" to proposition (2). He seems to be saying that in the short run administrative corruption contributes to the development of political parties, while in the long run these same parties that were built by corruption come to possess sufficient organized authority to foster the development of "organized group interests" in public policies, thereby under- mining the personal interests that nurture and sustain corruption.

It is not my purpose to comment on the historical aspects of the theory or the examples cited in support of it. It might be appropriate, however, to consider the two propositions from a conceptual point of view. Proposition (1) seems odd because it goes against our ordinary linguistic understanding of corruption and institutionalization as inversely related. It does not appear so unusual when we remember that the organ that is being corrupted [bureaucracy] is separate from the one being institutionalized [political party].** The validity of the proposition hinges on the establishment of an empirical linkage between its subject [bureaucratic corruption] and complement [party institutionaliza- tion], since there is no logical entailment. Some political parties have been built on a foundation of patronage (the American experience providing benchmark examples), but there is no self- evident reason for believing that politicians will invest their illegally diverted public funds for the capitalization and devel- opment of the political parties they lead. They may simply divert the funds to their own personal or familial uses, as past leaders of some defunct West African parties reportedly have done.[99] Even if they use the funds for party "patronage," there is no assurance that the patron-client relations thus nurtured will develop into the kind of structure that we would ordinarily denote by the term "organization." This has happened--e.g., in American political parties--but additional reasons would have to be adduced to indicate when and/or why it could (or could not) be expected to happen.

Proposition (2) involves the implication that the insti- tutionalization of political parties (and presumably other polit- ical associations) necessarily results in the depersonalization of relationships--denoted by such terms as "formalism," "procedur- alism," "officiality," etc.--as well as the collectivization (or collective treatment) of persons and their interests. It cannot be argued that such institutionalization necessarily reduces corruption--an empirical question--but presumably it encourages a view of political conduct which would tend to discourage cor- ruption by providing new standards for negatively evaluating such conduct (see pp. 68-70 below).

**It seems odd, nevertheless, to speak (as Harrington does, with Huntington's approval) of corruption as an alternative system of "government," which implies some conception of auth- ority, rather than as merely a method of political influence and personal interference, which includes no such implication. We can speak of a system of "patronage government" or of a cor- rupt system of government, but not of government as a system of corruption.

[99]Ronald Wraith and Edgar Simpkins, Corruption in Developing Countries (London: George Allen & Unwin, 1963), pp. 171-209; Victor T. LeVine, Political Corruption: The Ghana Case (Stanford: Hoover Institution Press, 1975).

James Scott has tried to show that corruption can contribute to the policy process, and hence to public government,
even as it undermines public administration.[100] He advances
three arguments in support of this contention. First, he argues
that "the corruption [c] of law enforcement [X] may be the most
efficient means of affecting changes [g] in de facto policy
[P]"; second, that corruption can contribute both to the enforcement [+] and nonenforcement [-] of policies; finally, that corruption may be the only way for excluded communities (e.g.,
"pariah capitalists" and commercial minorities such as the
Asians in East Africa or the Chinese in Southeast Asia) "to
safeguard their [collective] interests" [CI].

Before considering these propositions--each of them
entailed by Scott's conception of corruption as "political influence" exercised at the law- or policy-enforcement stage rather
than at the legislative or policymaking stage of the governmental
process--it is necessary to repeat an earlier observation that
by most definitions "policies" are de jure or authorized activities, making the term "de facto policy" (i.e., unauthorized
policy) a contradiction. It is therefore misleading to speak
of corruption in the first proposition,

$$(1) \quad cX \text{ contributes to } gP,$$

as an "efficient means of affecting changes in de facto policy."

Corruption could defeat a policy or it could contribute
to the enforcement of a policy, as suggested by proposition (2):

$$(2) \quad cX \text{ contributes to } \mp P.$$

It is conceivable that corruption could prompt the more effective
enforcement of a policy, or that it could force the abandonment
of a policy or its replacement by another one, but administrative
corruption at the enforcement stage cannot in any sense be a
substitute policy. Such corruption is not policymaking--it is
not the authorization of a plan, procedure, or activity by which
pre-selected categories of persons, actions, possessions, or
things are intended to be equitably and impartially dealt with.
(Only a type of corruption that penetrates government at the
legislative stage can issue in a policy, as we shall see below.)
Administrative corruption could become policy only if the cor-
rupter became the authority, but in that case he would not have
to resort to corruption. (We have already seen how this can
be the case with what Scott calls "parochial corruption," which

---

[100] Scott, pp. 24-25.

is not corruption at all but rather the honoring by officials
of anti-state obligations and their response to non-state
authorities.)

We have occasion here to catch a glimpse of the intimate
connection between the concepts of "authority" and "rules."[101]
Laws and policies authorize plans, procedures, and (ultimately)
official activities which, while they may be discretionary, must
always be justifiable in relation to some rule. At most, corruption may be "the rule"; it can never be, however widely and
routinely practiced, "a rule." The recurrent and persistent
corruption of a policy by officials prepared to charge the going
"price" for their indiscretion is not a substitute policy. The
only prices that conceivably could be regarded as consistent
with public policies are authorized administrative prices, such
as fees for public services, licenses, and so on.

The final proposition,

(3) cX contributes to CI,

that official corruption can safeguard the interests of excluded,
minority communities (CI), raises the conceptual problem of what
constitutes their "interests" and how corruption can contribute
to them. As it stands, the proposition would only seem to hold
if by CI is meant the sum of individual interests (II) of those
minority members in a position to corrupt officials and thereby
to safeguard their own private interests. Scott seems to mean
this, but also more than this, for he implies that CI can be
conceived as the aggregate of all II's within the minority
group--as the total interests of all members. Conceptually,
such interests could be dealt with individually by corruption,
though it is doubtful that all Kenyan Asians, for instance, are
individually capable of safeguarding their interests by such
means. Many Asian families have been unable to secure their
primary private interest by obtaining trading licenses from the
government, and have been forced not only out of business but
out of the country. This suggests that cX is an action that only
some individuals or families are capable of and that it can therefore contribute only to some II among members of a minority group.

Scott also seems to imply that cX is a collective strata-
gem available to minority groups--that cX can safeguard CI where
CI is a common interest of some kind. If CI was a commercial
minority's common interest, say, in freedom to participate in
the private sector of the economy without undue government

---

[101]Peter Winch, "Authority" in Anthony Quinton, ed., _Political
Philosophy_ (London: Oxford University Press, 1967), p. 100.

interference, then it is difficult to see how this CI could be
vouchsafed for all community members without a government law
or policy to that effect, as is the case with the minority
Chinese in Malaysia. (It should be emphasized that this is an
example of a CI--a communal interest--that can be responded to
appropriately by public policy because the minority in question
has a common private interest in economic policy derived from
its own economic specialization as a mercantile group.) But a
policy is not corruption. It is conceivable that such a CI
could be safeguarded if the minority were represented in government in some way--perhaps by a spokesman who defended their CI in
governing councils. Scott conceives of these minorities as being
excluded from government, however--their "political demands regarded as illegitimate by the governing elite and the general
population"; this certainly is the circumstance of Asians in
Kenya. In such a circumstance, the only way that cX could safeguard CI would be by the corruption of high policymaking offi-
cials--possibly the highest official--perhaps with bribes from
funds secured collectively by a self-imposed community tax or by
contributions from wealthier members made in behalf of the whole
community. Such bribery, cX, is consistent with both propositions
(1) and (2) by securing, in exchange for the bribe(s), an authoritative rule or action (P) that contributes to the collective
interest (CI) of the community (that collective interest already
having been defined, and having served as the basis upon which a
community tax was levied or fiduciary donations made). In this
case, cX would be regarded as bribery if the high official(s)
with the authority to provide the collective safeguard gained
personally from the exchange.

This would be perfectly consistent with Scott's argument
were it not for the fact that we are no longer analyzing the dynamics of corruption at the policy-enforcement stage of the governmental process. Rather, we are now considering the regime of
corruption at the legislative or policymaking stage. This, of
course, is the modal type of corruption in representative democracies, and more particularly in such institutions as legislatures
or committees where individual votes on proposed policies can be
bought, thereby influencing legislation and policymaking. Corruption in the U.S. Congress and its committees is typically of this
kind because of the independence of congressmen (unlike their
Parliamentary counterparts, who are quite closely controlled by
party whips and who therefore do not possess the individual authority that can be purchased by a bribe). To the extent that
governments in underdeveloped countries are not governed by independent legislatures and committees, such corruption is less likely than corruption at the enforcement stage. (There have been
recent reports indicating that the General Assembly of the United
Nations is an arena for this kind of political corruption in that
some members of poorer Third World delegations have been selling
their votes to richer delegations or wealthy third parties.)

Conclusion

These theories of Huntington and Scott aim at establishing links between corruption and public government at the organizational and behavioral levels of analysis. The linkages may also be theorized (I think more appropriately) at the normative level, especially since corruption is categorically a normative phenomenon. A normative analysis will consider the definition and evaluation of corruption in terms of their relationship to the social standards of particular reference groups.

Corruption is inherently a private relationship that thrives in the safety of secrecy, as it wilts in the light of publicity, because it is conduct in violation of accepted norms and laws. Even if corruption is not suspected, or is suspected but not verified, it is nevertheless possible to conceive of corruption and to evaluate hypothetical corrupt acts in the light of a society's or group's standards. The practice of corruption is impossible without a conception of what constitutes corrupt acts; so long as there are no standards, there can be no violation of them. In the absence of social standards, not only could we not speak of "corruption," we could not speak of "society," because society implies the existence of rules. The concept of corruption must be presumed to exist in all societies, although it is possible--but not very likely[102]--that corrupt conduct is not practiced in all societies. Thus a vocabulary of corruption will have utility in all politically organized societies, however upright their officials, because it is needed as a negative key to right conduct.

The character of corruption and its vocabulary will depend upon the social standards and reference group subscribed to by the evaluator. In contemporary underdeveloped countries, "official corruption" is widely believed to exist and has often been exposed by public inquiries. But the evaluations made by government inquiries conducted by lawyers may well be quite different from the evaluations made by ordinary persons who are more likely to identify with the rules and obligations of their communal groups than with the new state and its laws. We have seen that an act that is judged as "official corruption" from the standpoint of the new state may not be corruption at all when judged by communal standards. We also have seen that the corruption of official regulations is quite separate from the corruption of communal obligations--that the two kinds of corruption are categorically distinct.

---

[102]Carl Friedrich, The Pathology of Politics (New York: Harper & Row, 1972), p. 129.

CONCLUSION

The fact that we are able to conceive of different types
of corruption relating to different standards and reference
groups suggests a normative theory of political development that
in principle is verifiable. Concern about and condemnation of
particular kinds of corruption can signal the normative direc-
tion--and possibly the rate--of political change. If the misconduct prompting concern and condemnation is "social corruption,"
associated with a general indifference to "official corruption,"
then we know that the informal rules and obligations of the old
society remain the preeminent standard of conduct. If the misconduct prompting general concern is "official corruption," then
we know that the standards of the new state are being adopted
as the appropriate standards for evaluating political conduct.
(It is quite conceivable, even likely, that the levels of official and social corruption will both be high in societies
undergoing rapid social change, when norms and standards of all
kinds become uncertain or questionable.) Huntington views the
widespread practice of official corruption as "symptomatic of
the weakness of political institutions."[103] This is certainly
true, but if such corruption is generally condemned, and not
regarded with mere indifference or mild disapproval, we have
evidence that a normative process of political development has
taken place. Ceteris paribus, the more that official corruption
is condemned, the greater the validity of public government and
the new state in the eyes of a country's inhabitants.** Official
corruption, therefore, while symptomatic of the weakness of civic
institutions is--if condemned--also symptomatic of the growing
value attached to such institutions, of the normative tension
between new standards and existing performances and practices.
Indeed, it is symptomatic of the "modernization" of political
morality.

Political modernization, in this normative analysis,
entails not the reduction or elimination of corruption (a
practical problem in any moral order), but rather the adoption
of a particular conception of it--specifically the modern

---

[103]Huntington, p. 63.

**Such evaluations should be susceptible to empirical anal-
ysis--for instance, by means of attitude surveys. Indeed,
survey research would seem to be a particularly appropriate
technique for investigating conflict and change in the nature
of public and para-public morals in developing countries. Therefore, the normative theory of political development proposed
herein is probably verifiable not only in principle but also in
practice. (There may of course be political and cultural obstacles to the carrying out of such surveys, but that is a
separate, tactical issue.)

conception of "official corruption." Recent experiences in North American and European countries serve to remind us that official corruption, and other abuses of public authority, are far from absent in modern governments. But the widespread condemnation of such practices, where they have been exposed, indicates the vitality of the modern standards of public probity in these same countries. In many underdeveloped countries, it is not only this degree of public concern that is lacking, but also the conception of misconduct it rests upon.

BIBLIOGRAPHY

Aboyade, Ojetunji. "Relations Between Central and Local Institutions in the Development Process." In Rivkin, ed.

Abrams, Philip. The Origins of British Sociology, 1834-1914. Chicago: University of Chicago Press, 1968.

Aikin, Charles. "Corruption." In Gould and Kolb, eds.

Almond, Gabriel, and Coleman, James S., eds. The Politics of the Developing Areas. Princeton: Princeton University Press, 1960.

Anderson, Eugene, and Anderson, Pauline. Political Institutions and Social Change in Continental Europe in the Nineteenth Century. Berkeley: University of California Press, 1967.

Aron, Raymond. Main Currents in Sociological Thought. 2 vols. New York: Basic Books, 1965.

Barker, Ernest. Principles of Social and Political Theory. New York: Oxford University Press, 1961.

Barry, Brian. Political Argument. London: Routledge & Kegan Paul, 1965.

Barth, Fredrik, ed. Ethnic Groups and Boundaries. Boston: Little, Brown, 1969.

Beer, Samuel. British Politics in the Collectivist Age. New York: Alfred A. Knopf, 1965.

_____. Modern Political Development. New York: Random House, 1974.

Bendix, Reinhard. Max Weber: An Intellectual Portrait. New York: Anchor Books, 1962.

_____. "Social Stratification and the Political Community." In Laslett and Runciman, eds.

_____, and Roth, Guenther. Scholarship and Partisanship: Essays on Max Weber. Berkeley: University of California Press, 1971.

Bolingbroke, Viscount. Political Writings. Ed. Isaac Kramnick. New York: Appleton-Century-Crofts, 1970.

Bone, Hugh. "Patronage." In Gould and Kolb, eds.

Deutsch, Karl. The Nerves of Government. New York: The Free Press, 1966.

Easton, David. _A Framework for Political Analysis._ Englewood Cliffs: Prentice-Hall, 1965.

_____. _A Systems Analysis of Political Life._ New York: Wiley, 1965.

Fischer, Wolfram, and Lundgreen, Peter. "The Recruitment and Training of Administrative and Technical Personnel." In Tilly, ed.

Friedrich, Carl. _The Pathology of Politics._ New York: Harper & Row, 1972.

_____. _Tradition and Authority._ London: Pall Mall Press, 1972.

_____, ed. _Nomos VII: Rational Decision._ New York: Atherton, 1967.

Furnivall, J.S. _Netherlands India._ Cambridge: Cambridge University Press, 1939.

Geertz, Clifford, ed. _Old Societies and New States._ New York: The Free Press, 1963.

Gerth, H., and Mills, C. Wright, eds. _From Max Weber: Essays in Sociology._ New York: Oxford University Press, 1958.

Gertzel, Cherry, Goldschmidt, Maure, and Rothchild, Donald, eds. _Government and Politics in Kenya._ Nairobi: East African Publishing House, 1969.

Glazer, Nathan. _Affirmative Discrimination: Ethnic Inequality and Public Policy._ New York: Basic Books, 1975.

_____, and Moynihan, Daniel, eds., _Ethnicity: Theory and Experience._ Cambridge, Mass.: Harvard University Press, 1975.

Gould, Julius, and Kolb, William, eds. _A Dictionary of the Social Sciences._ New York: The Free Press, 1964.

Hanna, William, and Hanna, Judith, eds. _Urban Dynamics in Black Africa._ Chicago: Aldine-Atherton, 1971.

Hansard Society. _Problems of Parliamentary Government in Colonies._ London: Hansard Society, 1953.

_____. _What Are the Problems of Parliamentary Government in West Africa?_ London: Hansard Society, 1958.

Harrison, Wilfred. "Policy." In Gould and Kolb, eds.

Hart, H.L.A. _The Concept of Law._ Oxford: The Clarendon Press, 1961.

Hayek, Friedrich. _The Constitution of Liberty._ Chicago: University of Chicago Press, 1960.

_____. _Law, Legislation and Liberty._ Chicago: University of Chicago Press, 1973. Vol. 1: _Rules and Order._

BIBLIOGRAPHY

Hirschman, A.O. Voice, Exit and Loyalty. Cambridge, Mass.: Harvard University Press, 1970.

Huntington, Samuel. Political Order in Changing Societies. New Haven: Yale University Press, 1968.

Kirkwood, Kenneth, ed. African Affairs, Number 10. London: Chatto & Windus, 1961.

Kuper, Leo, and Smith, M.G., eds. Pluralism in Africa. Berkeley: University of California Press, 1971.

Landé, Carl. Leaders, Factions and Parties. Monograph Series, No. 6, Southeast Asia Studies, Yale University, 1966.

Laslett, Peter. The World We Have Lost. New York: Charles Scribners and Sons, 1965.

_____, and Runciman, W.G., eds. Philosophy, Politics and Society. 2nd Ser. Oxford: Basil Blackwell, 1962.

LeVine, Victor T. Political Corruption: The Ghana Case. Stanford: Hoover Institution Press, 1975.

Lewis, I.M. "The Politics of the 1969 Somali Coup," Journal of Modern African Studies, Vol. 10 (October 1972), pp. 383-408.

Lindblom, Charles E. The Intelligence of Democracy. New York: The Free Press, 1965.

_____. The Policy-Making Process. Englewood Cliffs: Prentice-Hall, 1968.

Long, Norton. "Public Policy and Administration: The Goals of Rationality and Responsibility," Public Administration Review, Vol. XIV (Winter 1954), pp. 22-31.

Mansfield, Harvey C., Jr. "Rationality and Representation in Burke's 'Bristol Speech.'" In Friedrich, ed., pp. 197-216.

Mboya, Tom. The Challenge of Nationhood. London: Andre Deutsch, 1970.

Merton, Robert K. Social Theory and Social Structure. Glencoe: The Free Press, 1957.

Mill, John Stuart. Utilitarianism; On Liberty; and Considerations on Representative Government. London: J.M. Dent, 1910.

Milne, R.S. "Decision-Making in Developing Countries," Journal of Comparative Administration, Vol. 4 (February 1972).

Minogue, K.R. Nationalism. Baltimore: Penguin Books, 1970.

Myrdal, Gunnar. Asian Drama: An Inquiry into the Poverty of Nations. 3 vols. Harmondsworth: Penguin Books, 1968.

Nagel, Thomas. "Equal Treatment and Compensatory Discrimination," Philosophy and Public Affairs, Vol. 2 (Summer 1973), pp. 348-63.

Nisbet, Robert. The Sociological Tradition. London: Heinemann, 1966.

Nye, Joseph S. "Corruption and Political Development: A Cost-Benefit Analysis," American Political Science Review, Vol. LXI (June 1967), pp. 417-27.

Oakeshott, Michael. On Human Conduct. Oxford: The Clarendon Press, 1975.

Olson, Mancur. The Logic of Collective Action. Cambridge, Mass.: Harvard University Press, 1965.

Parris, Henry. Constitutional Bureaucracy. London: George Allen & Unwin, 1969.

Pennock, J. Roland, and Chapman, John, eds. Nomos XI: Voluntary Association. New York: Atherton Press, 1969.

Plamenatz, J.P. "Interest (Political Science)." In Gould and Kolb, eds.

Plumb, J.H. The Growth of Political Stability in England: 1675-1725. Harmondsworth: Penguin Books, 1969.

Quinton, Anthony, ed. Political Philosophy. London: Oxford University Press, 1967.

Rivkin, Arnold, ed. Nations by Design. New York: Anchor Books, 1968.

Roth, Guenther. "Personal Rulership, Patrimonialism, and Empire-Building." In Bendix and Roth.

Ryan, Alan. "Utilitarianism and Bureaucracy: The Views of J.S. Mill." In Sutherland, ed.

Scott, James C. Comparative Political Corruption. Englewood Cliffs: Prentice-Hall, 1972.

Singer, Peter. "Famine, Affluence and Morality," Philosophy and Public Affairs, Vol. 1 (Spring 1972), pp. 229-43.

Sutherland, Gilliam, ed. Studies in the Growth of Nineteenth-Century Government. London: Routledge & Kegan Paul, 1972.

Thomson, Judith. "Preferential Hiring," Philosophy and Public Affairs, Vol. 2 (Summer 1973), pp. 364-84.

Tilly, Charles, ed. The Formation of National States in Western Europe. Princeton: Princeton University Press, 1975.

Titmus, Richard M. Social Policy. New York: Pantheon Books, 1974.

INSTITUTE OF INTERNATIONAL STUDIES
UNIVERSITY OF CALIFORNIA, BERKELEY

CARL G. ROSBERG,
Director

Monographs published by the Institute include:

RESEARCH SERIES

1. *The Chinese Anarchist Movement*, by Robert A. Scalapino and George T. Yu. ($1.00)
3. *Land Tenure and Taxation in Nepal*, Volume I, *The State as Landlord: Raikar Tenure*, by Mahesh C. Regmi. ($8.75; unbound photocopy)
4. *Land Tenure and Taxation in Nepal*, Volume II, *The Land Grant System: Birta Tenure*, by Mahesh C. Regmi. ($2.50)
*5. *Mexico and Latin American Economic Integration*, by Philippe C. Schmitter and Ernst B. Haas. ($1.00)
6. *Local Taxation in Tanganyika*, by Eugene C. Lee. ($1.00)
7. *Birth Rates in Latin America: New Estimates of Historical Trends*, by O. Andrew Collver. ($2.50)
8. *Land Tenure and Taxation in Nepal*, Volume III, *The Jagir, Rakam, and Kipat Tenure Systems*, by Mahesh C. Regmi. ($2.50)
9. *Ecology and Economic Development in Tropical Africa*, edited by David Brokensha. ($8.25; unbound photocopy)
10. *Urban Areas in Indonesia: Administrative and Census Concepts*, by Pauline Dublin Milone. ($10.50; unbound photocopy)
11. *Cultural Processes in the Baltic Area under Soviet Rule*, by Stephen P. Dunn. ($1.25)
12. *Land Tenure and Taxation in Nepal*, Volume IV, *Religious and Charitable Land Endowments: Guthi Tenure*, by Mahesh C. Regmi. ($2.75)
13. *The Pink Yo-Yo: Occupational Mobility in Belgrade, ca. 1915-1965*, by Eugene A. Hammel. ($2.00)
14. *Community Development in Israel and the Netherlands: A Comparative Analysis*, by Ralph M. Kramer. ($2.50)
*15. *Central American Economic Integration: The Politics of Unequal Benefits*, by Stuart I. Fagan. ($2.00)
16. *The International Imperatives of Technology: Technological Development and the International Political System*, by Eugene B. Skolnikoff. ($2.95)
*17. *Autonomy or Dependence as Regional Integration Outcomes: Central America*, by Philippe C. Schmitter. ($1.75)
18. *Framework for a General Theory of Cognition and Choice*, by Robert M. Axelrod. ($1.50)
19. *Entry of New Competitors in Yugoslav Market Socialism*, by Stephen R. Sacks. ($2.50)
*20. *Political Integration in French-Speaking Africa*, by Abdul A. Jalloh. ($3.50)
21. *The Desert and the Sown: Nomads in the Wider Society*, edited by Cynthia Nelson. ($3.50)
22. *U.S.-Japanese Competition in International Markets: A Study of the Trade-Investment Cycle in Modern Capitalism*, by John E. Roemer. ($3.95)
23. *Political Disaffection Among British University Students: Concepts, Measurement, and Causes*, by Jack Citrin and David J. Elkins. ($2.00)
24. *Urban Inequality and Housing Policy in Tanzania: The Problem of Squatting*, by Richard E. Stren. ($2.50)
*25. *The Obsolescence of Regional Integration Theory*, by Ernst B. Haas. ($2.95)

*International Integration Series

26. *The Voluntary Service Agency in Israel*, by Ralph M. Kramer. ($2.00)
27. *The SOCSIM Demographic-Sociological Microsimulation Program: Operating Manual*, by Eugene A. Hammel *et al.* ($4.50)
28. *Authoritarian Politics in Communist Europe: Uniformity & Diversity in One-Party States*, edited by Andrew C. Janos. ($3.75)

29. *The Anglo-Icelandic Cod War of 1972-1973:   A Case Study of a Fishery Dispute*, by Jeffrey A. Hart. ($2.00)

POLITICS OF MODERNIZATION SERIES

1. *Spanish Bureaucratic-Patrimonialism in America*, by Magali Sarfatti. ($2.00)
2. *Civil-Military Relations in Argentina, Chile, and Peru*, by Liisa North. ($1.75)
3. *Notes on the Process of Industrialization in Argentina, Chile, and Peru*, by Alcira Leiserson. ($1.75)
4. *Chilean Christian Democracy: Politics and Social Forces*, by James Petras. ($1.50)
5. *Social Stratification in Peru*, by Magali Sarfatti Larson and Arlene Eisen Bergman. ($4.95)
6. *Modernization and Coercion*, by Mario Barrera. ($1.50)
7. *Latin America: The Hegemonic Crisis and the Military Coup*, by José Nun. (2.00)
8. *Developmental Processes in Chilean Local Government*, by Peter S. Cleaves. ($1.50)
9. *Modernization and Bureaucratic-Authoritarianism: Studies in South American Politics*, by Guillermo A. O'Donnell. ($3.50)

WORKING PAPERS ON DEVELOPMENT

1. *Indian Economic Policy and Performance: A Framework for a Progressive Society*, by Jagdish N. Bhagwati. ($1.00)
2. *Toward a Comparative Study of Revolutions*, by Elbaki Hermassi. ($1.50)
3. *Patrons, Clients, and Politicians: New Perspectives on Political Clientelism*, by Keith R. Legg. ($2.00)